# Mount Pleasant, Newport, Onondaga, Middleport Ontario in Colour Photos, Saving Our History One Photo at a Time

Photography
by Barbara Raué
2017

Series Name:
Cruising Ontario

Book 184

Cover photo: 637 Mount Pleasant Road, Page 27

# Series Name: Cruising Ontario
## Saving Our History One Photo at a Time in colour photos

Books Available in Alphabetical Order:
Aberfoyle, Acton, Alton, Amherstburg, Ancaster, Arthur, Aylmer, Ayr, Bloomingdale, Brantford, Burlington, Caledon, Caledonia, Cambridge, Clifford, Conestogo, Delhi, Dorchester to Aylmer, Drayton, Drumbo, Dundas, Eden Mills, Elmira, Elora, Essex, Fergus, Guelph, Hagersville, Hamilton, Hanover, Harriston, Hespeler, Jarvis, Kingston, Kingsville, Kitchener, Linwood, Listowel, London, Lucknow, Mono, Mount Forest, Neustadt, New Hamburg, Niagara-on-the-Lake, Oakville, Orangeville, Orillia, Owen Sound, Palmerston, Peterborough, Petrolia, Port Elgin, Preston, Rockwood, Sarnia, Seaforth, Sheffield, Shelburne, Simcoe, Southampton, St. Jacobs, St. Marys, St. Thomas, Stoney Creek, Stratford, Thamesford, Tillsonburg, Waterdown, Waterford, Waterloo, Welland, Wellesley, Windsor, Wingham, Woodstock

Book 157: Brockville
Book 158: Merrickville
Book 159: Smiths Falls
Book 160: Portland, Newboro
Book 161: Westport & Area
Book 162: Perth
Book 163-166: Belleville
Book 167-168: Port Colborne
Book 169: Erin in Colour
Book 170: Goderich in Colour
Book 171: Sault Ste. Marie
Book 172: Lake Superior
Book 173-176: Thunder Bay
Book 177-179: Paris

Book 180-181: St. George
Book 182-183: Burford
Book 184: Mt Pleasant, Onondaga, Newport

# Other Books by Barbara Raue

Coins of Gold

Arrows, Indians and Love

The Life and Times of Barbara
Volume 1: Inventions That Have Enhanced My Life
Volume 2: Entertainment That I Have Enjoyed
Volume 3: East Coast Trips
Volume 4: Olympics Have Always Intrigued Me
Volume 5: Wonders of the World
Volume 6: Caribbean Cruises We Have Enjoyed
Volume 7: Animals
Volume 8: Storms and Other Major Disasters in My Lifetime
Volume 9: Wars, Terrorist Attacks and Major Disasters

The Cromwell Family Book

Laura Secord Discovered

Daddy Where Are You?

Montana Series
Book 1: Montana Dream
Book 2: Life on the Montana Frontier
Book 3: Montana to Boston and Back
Book 4: Montana Sons Go to War
Book 5: Montana Sons Return From War

Visit Barbara's website to view all of her books
http://barbararaue.ca

Table of Contents

Township of Brantford

    Mount Pleasant                    Page 8

    Newport                          Page 34

Township of Onondaga

    Village of Onondaga          Page 40

    Village of Middleport         Page 50

Architectural Terms                Page 65

Building Styles                       Page 69

## Township of Brantford

Brantford Township was the largest and most central township of Brant County. The first area settled was along Fairchild's Creek north west of Cainsville. The township was blessed with many creeks that were developed with mills. The first industrial operation in the township was a mill operated by James Percy in Mount Pleasant. The township also has fertile soil and land was quickly settled and within twenty-five years was well under cultivation and thriving. Within the township are the villages of Mount Pleasant, Burtch, Newport, Cainsville and Langford, as well as the homes of Alexander Graham Bell and George Brown, a father of confederation.

Within decades of its founding in 1799 by the Ellis and Sturgis families, Mount Pleasant was a prosperous and cultured settlement with flourishing farms, inns, mills, schools, a drill hall, and commercial establishments. Today Mount Pleasant's long and lovely main street retains much of its rural charm and many of its old homes, churches, and farmsteads. Mount Pleasant Road is part of the Long Point Trail, an old Indian trail which went from the Grand River in Brantford south to Lake Erie.

Emily Stowe was the first woman to practice medicine in Canada and also the first woman school principal. After her marriage in 1856 to carriage-maker John Stowe, she taught at the renowned Nelles Academy at 667 Mount Pleasant Road. She studied medicine in the United States because she was refused admission to a Canadian medical school. She did a lot of campaigning for increased education opportunities for women, and her daughter, Augusta Stowe Gullen, born in Mount Pleasant in 1857, became the first woman to graduate in medicine from a Canadian university in 1883.

One of the earliest settlers in the area of Newport was Edee Burtch who purchased land from Joseph Brant around 1796. As more settlers arrived, the area became known as Burtch's Landing and was later renamed Newport. Newport was laid out for settlement by Thaddeus Smith in 1857. Newport was a thriving shipping port offering passenger service to Buffalo on the Red Jacket and Queen paddle wheel steamers that operated on the Grand River. There were also facilities for handling general freight. The village with several hundred people had two wagon and carriage shops, two blacksmith shops, brickyards, several general stores, a post office, two churches, a school, a tavern/ hotel, a sawmill, grain warehouses and a grist mill.

## Township of Onondaga

The township was named for the Onondagas, a nation within the Six Nations. They settled on land granted to the Six Nations under the Haldimand Proclamation of 1784. The Grand River, which forms the southern boundary of the county of Brant, was the main artery for transportation, communication, and economic sustenance. Today this river is mainly used for recreation. In the 1830s settlers began moving into this rich agricultural area.

This Village of Onondaga was first known as Smith's Corners for David Smith who operated a grocery store and a saloon. The name was later changed to Onondaga. The village became a thriving community in the mid-19th century because of the Buffalo, Brantford, and Goderich Railway station located here. Schools, churches, hotels and taverns, grist and sawmills, blacksmith shops, stores and small manufacturing shops developed.

The Grand River Navigation Company played an important role in the establishment of the Village of Middleport. On November 7, 1848 navigation was opened on the Grand River from Brantford to Dunnville through a series of locks and dams. Middleport, founded by John Solomon Hager, was midway between the locks at Brantford and the Village of Caledonia making it an important port.

**Mount Pleasant**

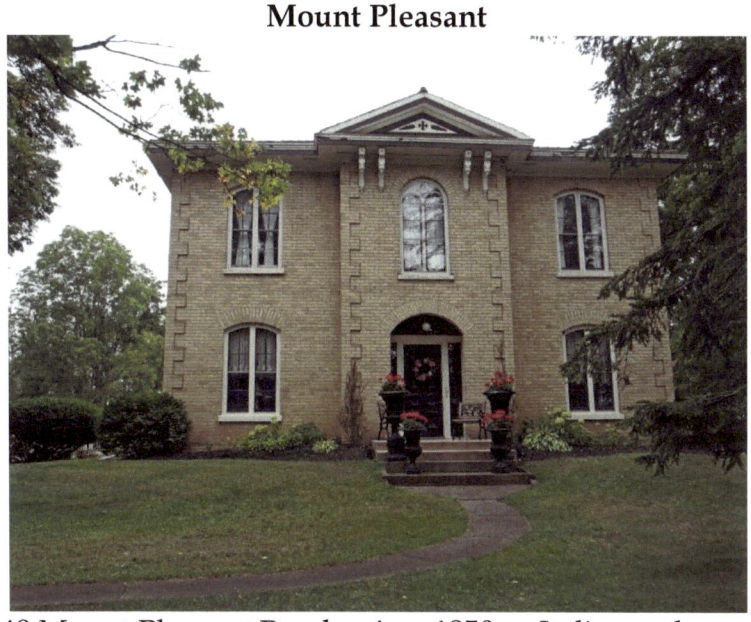

849 Mount Pleasant Road – circa 1850s – Italianate home – Archibald McEwen, a prosperous farmer and merchant, had a store on the same property.

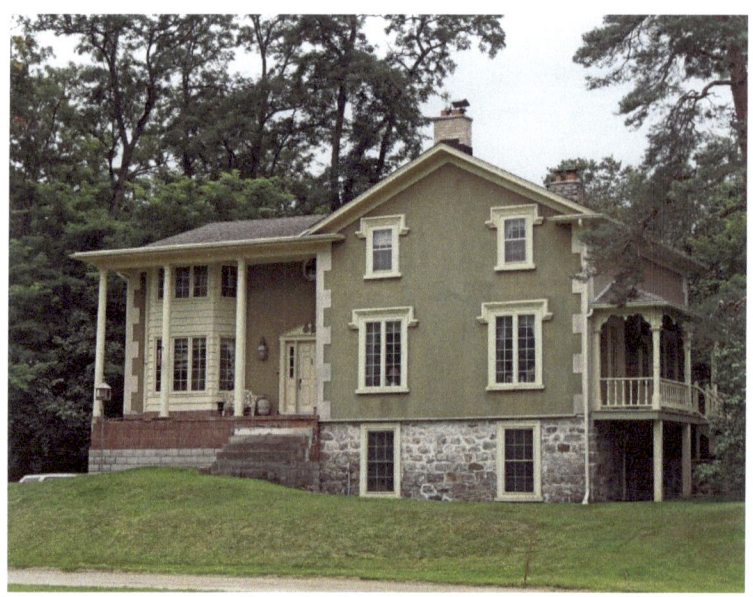

756 Mount Pleasant Road – Eadie-Wilson Home 'Idylbrook' – 1850 – at one time a stagecoach stop for coaches to and from Port Dover

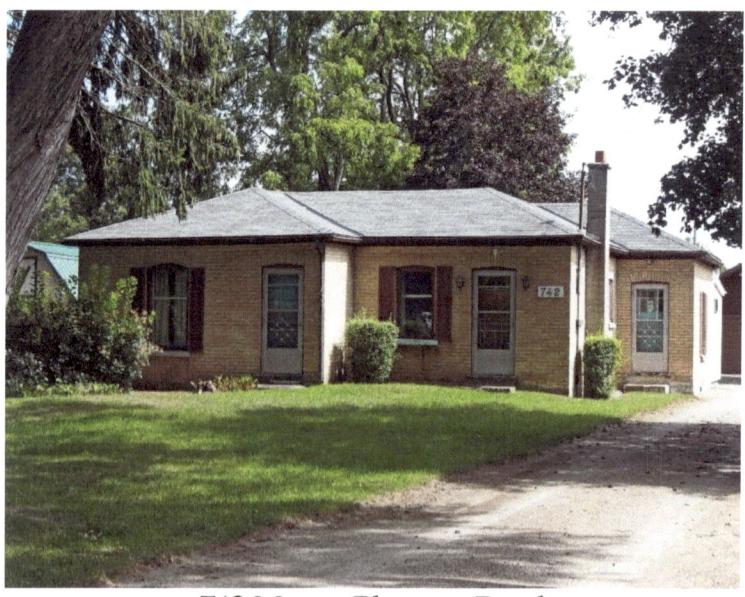

742 Mount Pleasant Road

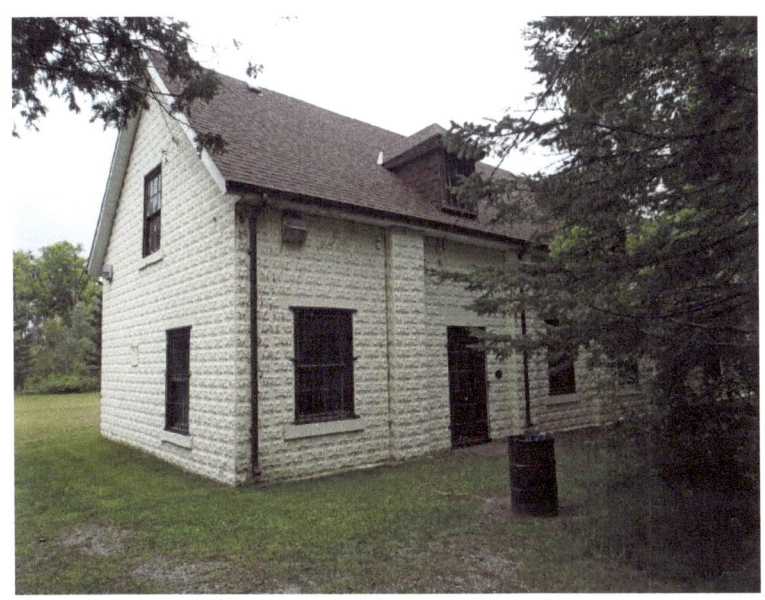

755 Mount Pleasant Road –
About 1842, Elijah Haight built a grist and carding mill using water from the Mount Pleasant Creek to power the mill. The new mill pond was popular with the local boys for trout fishing and swimming. The mill was demolished in 1911 when the property became the Ontario Ministry of Natural Resources first fish hatchery. The hatchery building and rearing ponds were constructed then. Mount Pleasant Nature Park is now operated by the local Optimist Club. The park is twenty-three acres, and has three large ponds.

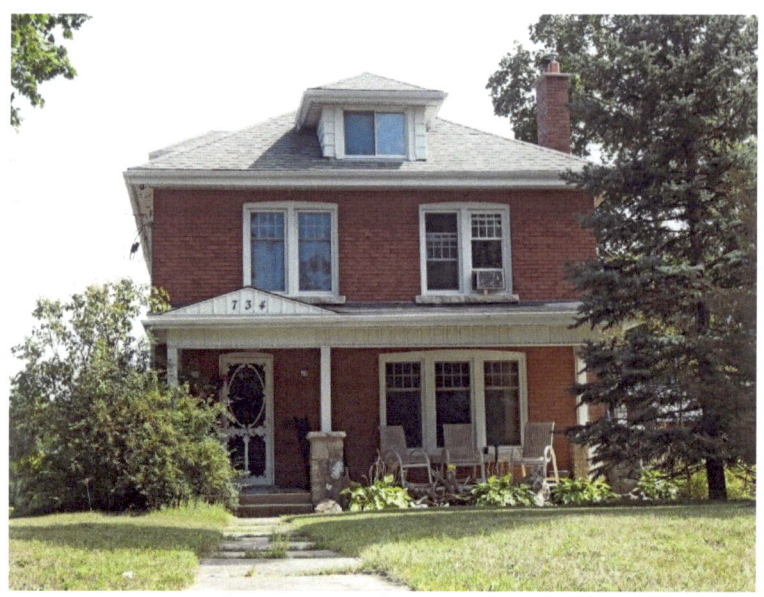

734 Mount Pleasant Road

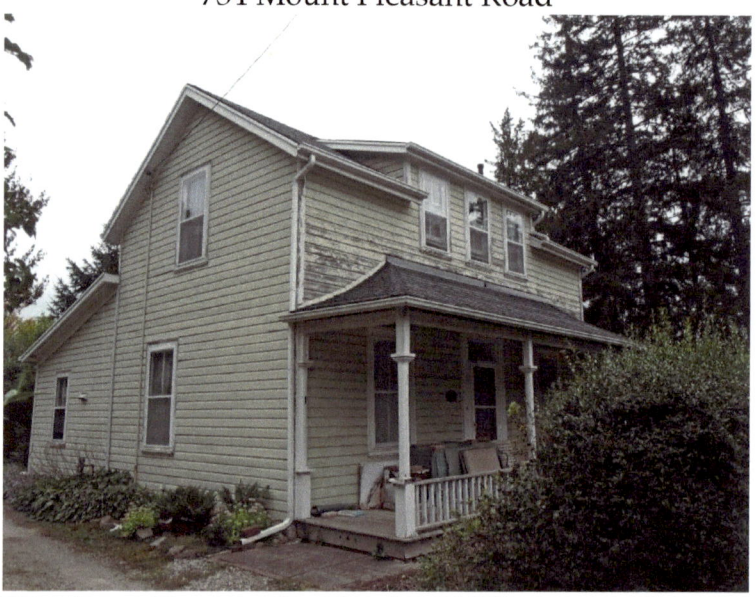

726 Mount Pleasant Road – circa 1870s – Owned by Dr. Duncan Marquis, a highly-regarded local doctor, this charming vernacular frame house in the unusual dormer style was probably built in the 1870s and is essentially unaltered.

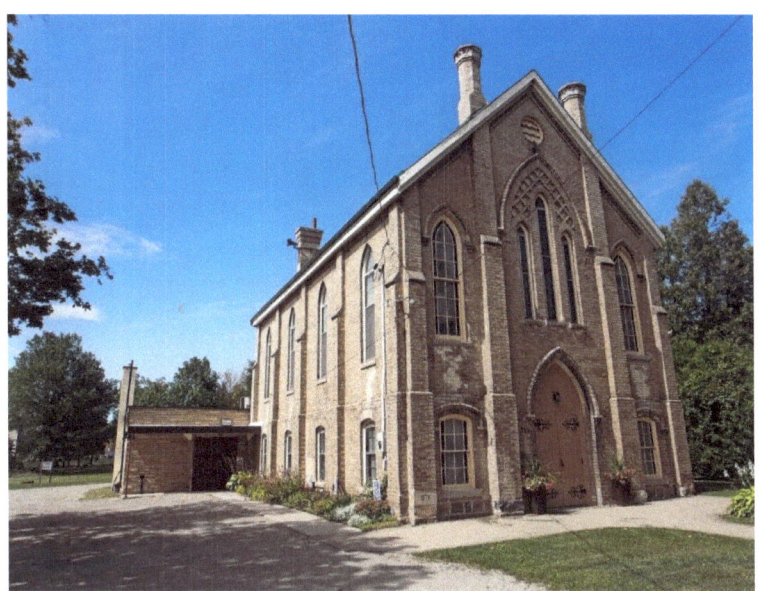

715 Mount Pleasant Road – Presbyterian Church – Victorian Gothic built in 1878 – The front façade features three lancet windows framed by a single molding accented by lattice brickwork above.

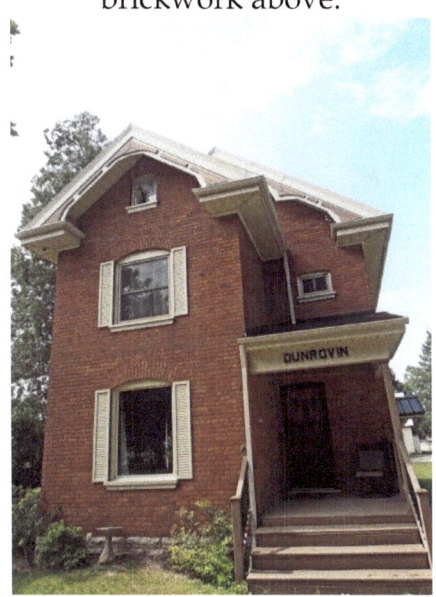

713 Mount Pleasant Road – 'Dunrovin'

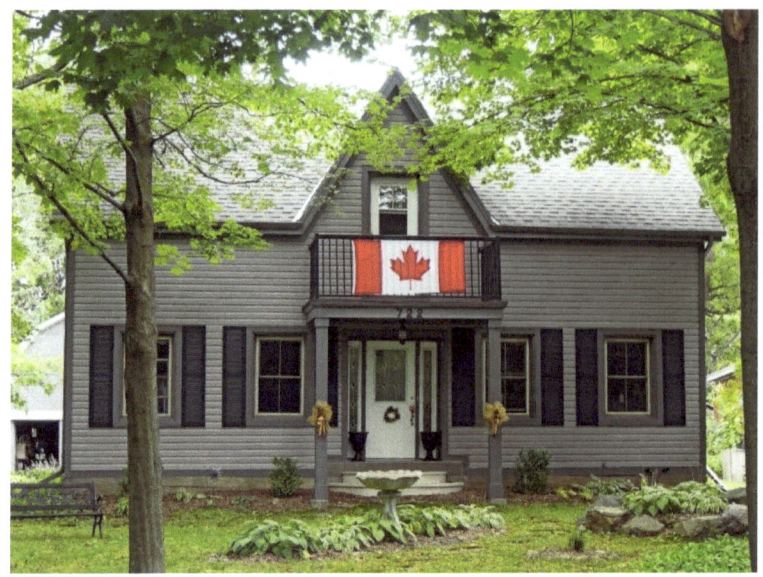

722 Mount Pleasant Road – Grantham House, circa 1840, is a vernacular farmhouse with eighteen inch thick walls composed of a clay, straw and mud mixture applied between horizontal planks. There are sidelights on the front door.

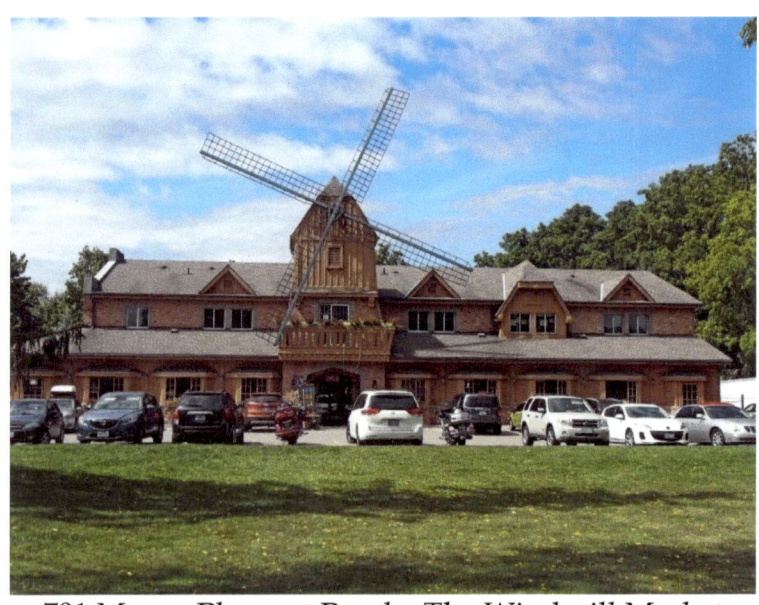

701 Mount Pleasant Road – The Windmill Market

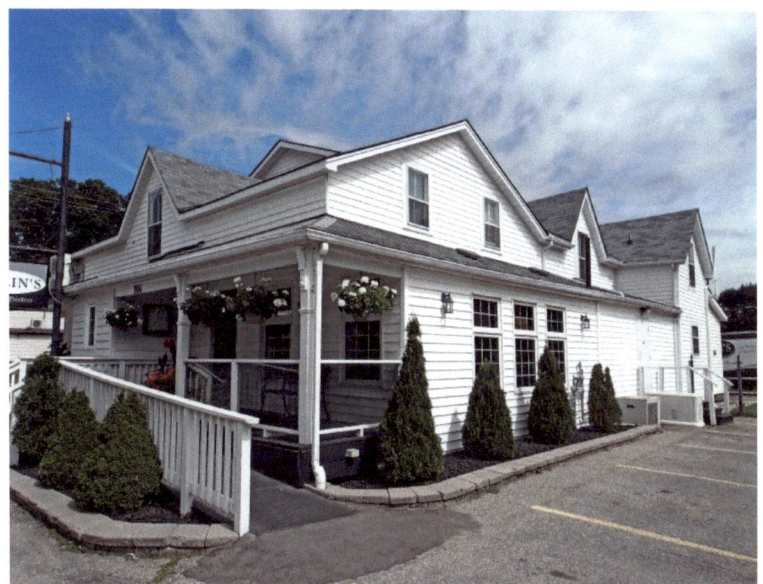

704 Mount Pleasant Road – Devlin's Country Bistro – 1834 – This Neo-Gothic former general store and post office has been a landmark in the village since it was built in 1834. It is the birthplace of Arthur Sturgis Hardy, a prominent lawyer and the fourth Premier of Ontario.

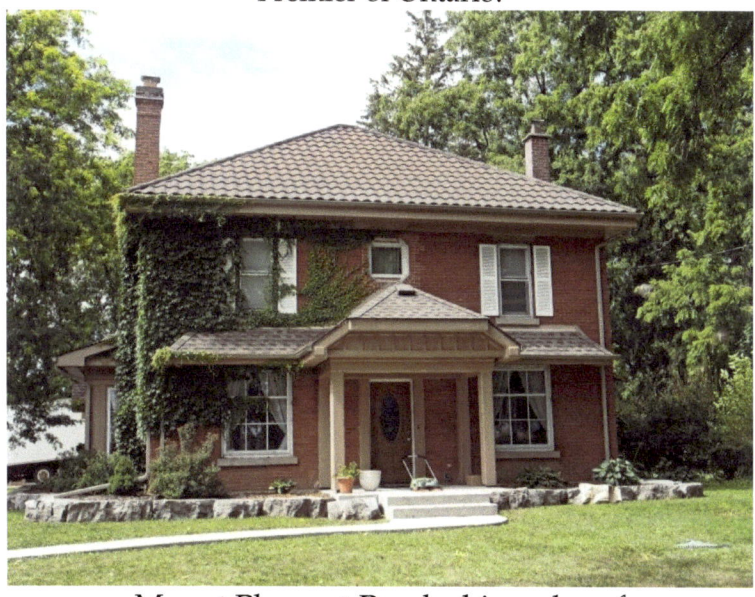

Mount Pleasant Road – hipped roof

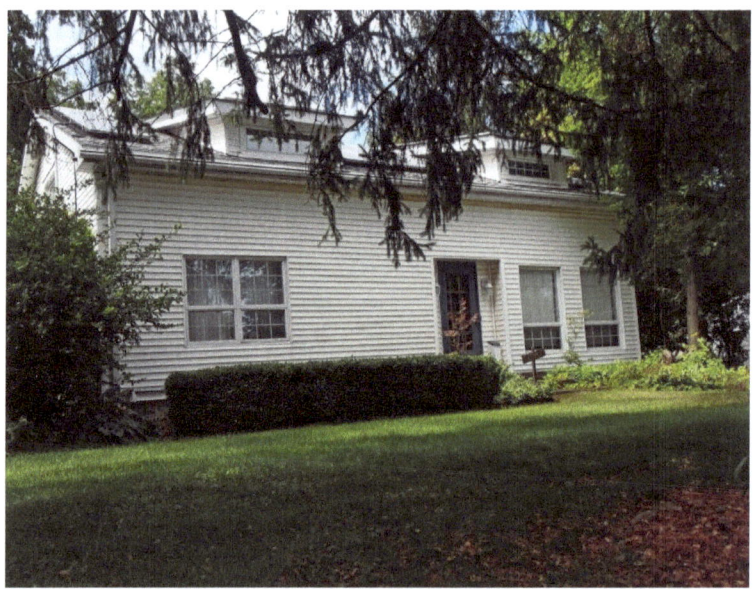
693 Mount Pleasant Road - dormers

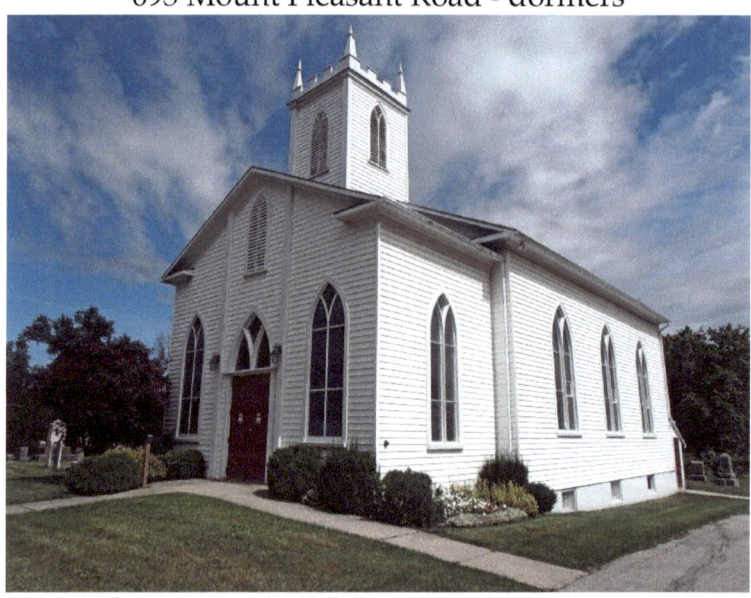
688 Mount Pleasant Road – All Saints Anglican Church was erected in 1845 by the parishioners using lumber from the local forest. There are lancet windows with muntins, cornice return on the gable, and a tower with finials and battlementing.

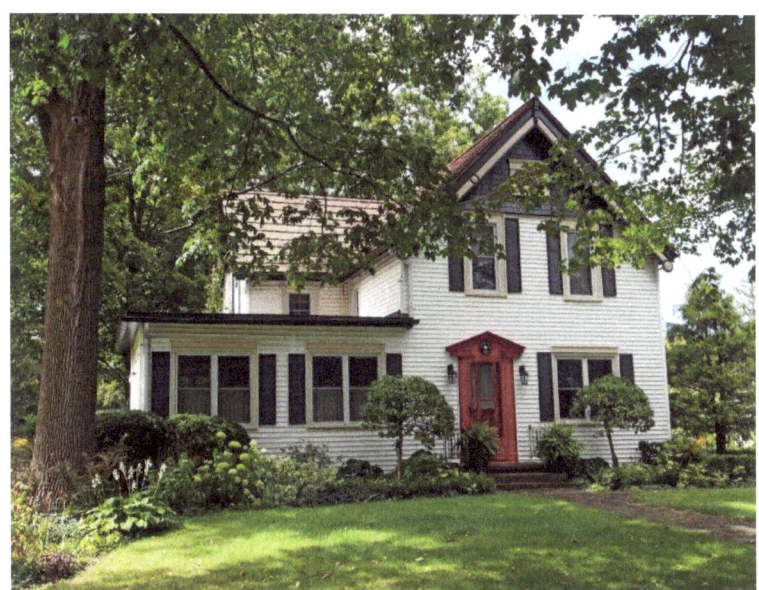

683 Mount Pleasant Road

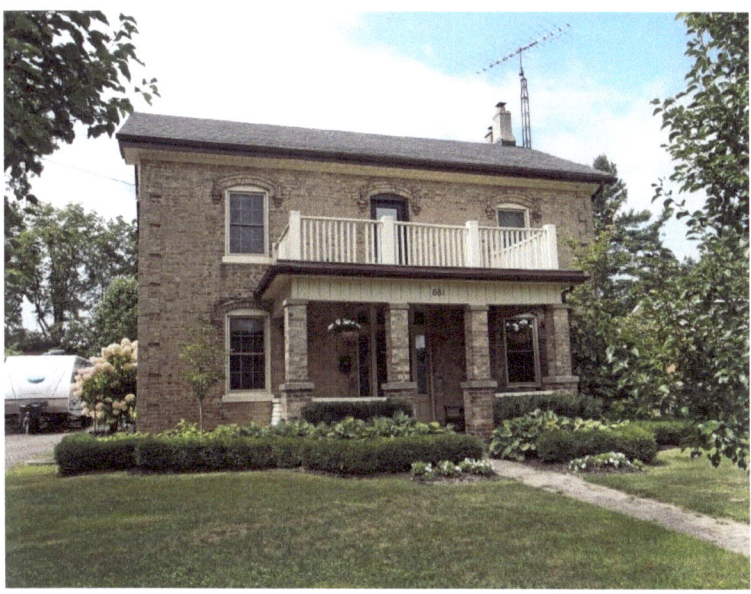

681 Mount Pleasant Road – United Church Manse – circa 1885 – plain Georgian styling with hooded molds over the windows, corner quoins, second floor balcony

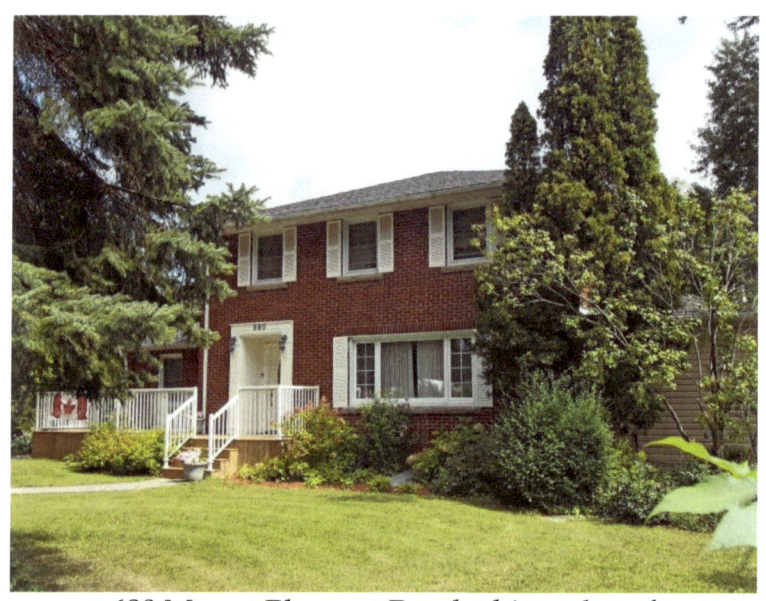

680 Mount Pleasant Road – hipped roof

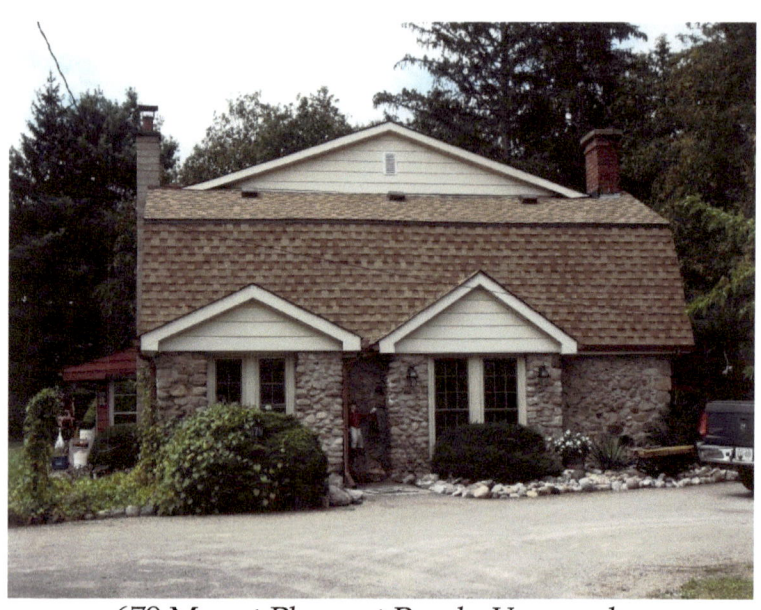

679 Mount Pleasant Road - Vernacular

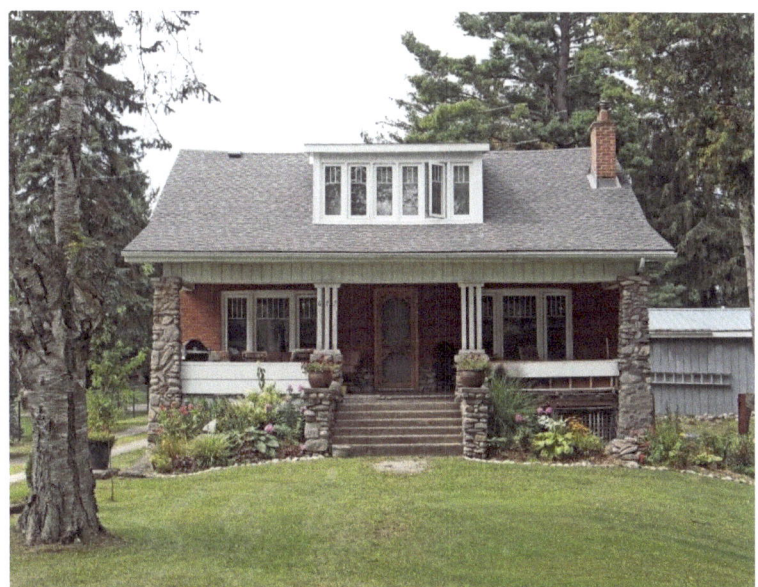

677 Mount Pleasant Road - dormer

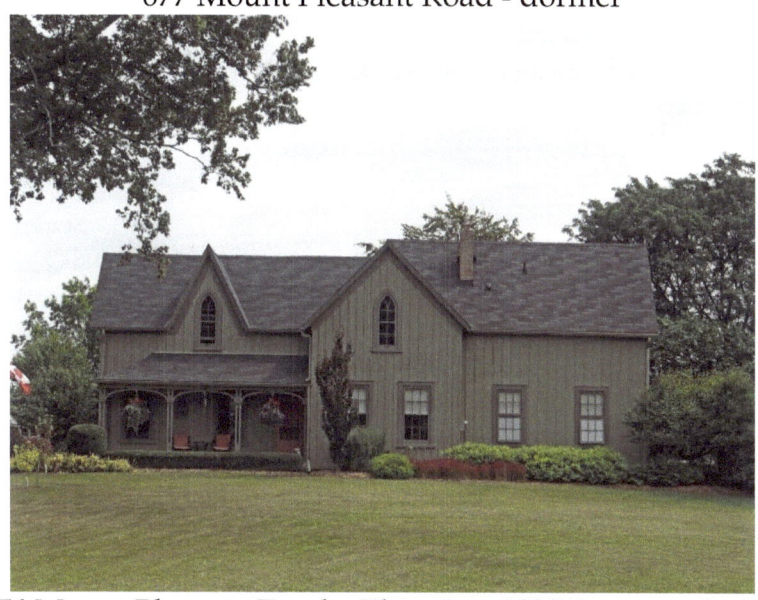

676 Mount Pleasant Road – This circa 1830 Regency Gothic cottage was the manse of the first Presbyterian and resident minister in the village, Reverend John Bryning – board and batten construction.

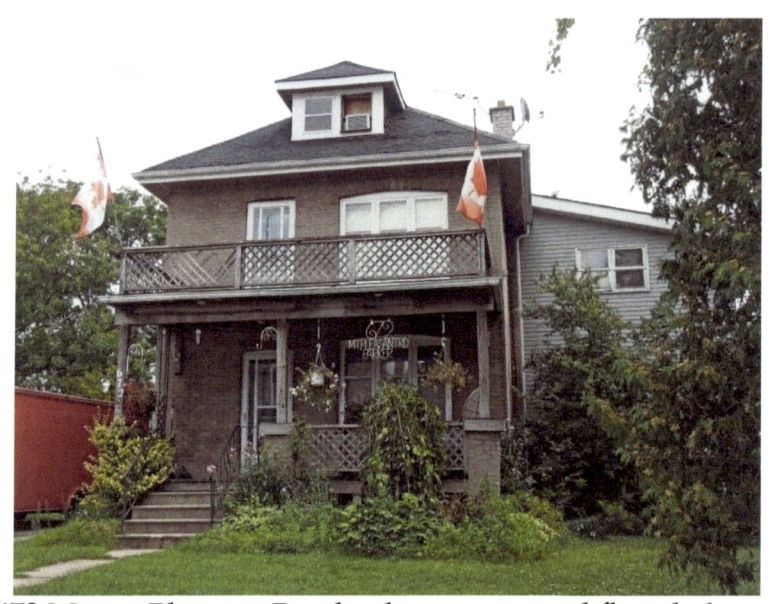
672 Mount Pleasant Road – dormer, second floor balcony

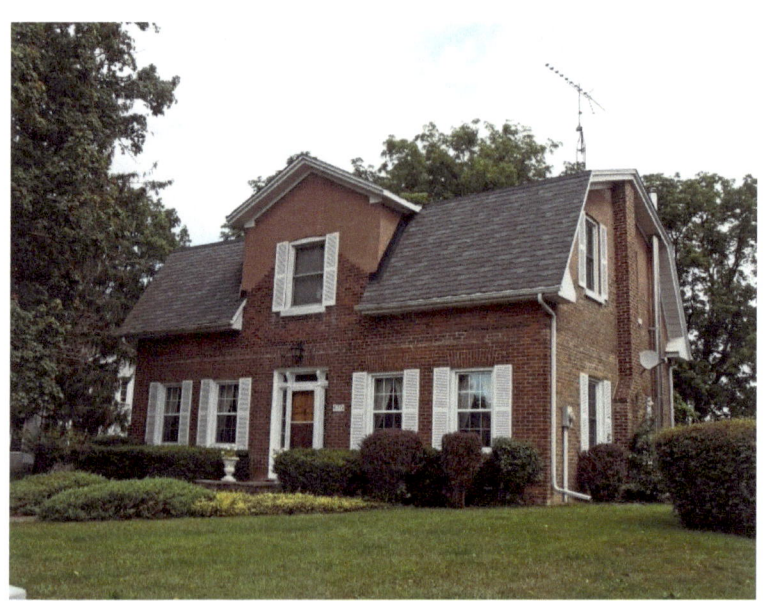
670 Mount Pleasant Road – Neo-Colonial – gambrel roof

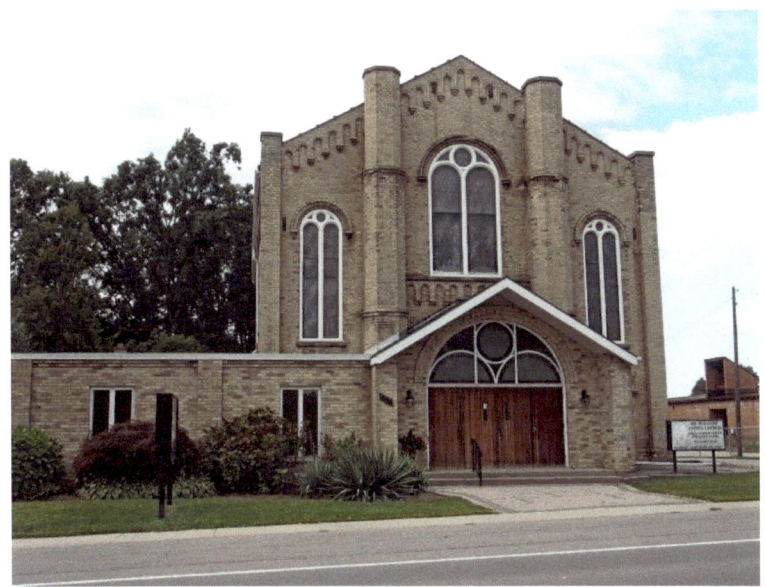

669 Mount Pleasant Road – United Church – built in 1858 by the Wesleyan Methodist congregation in the Italianate style in white brick

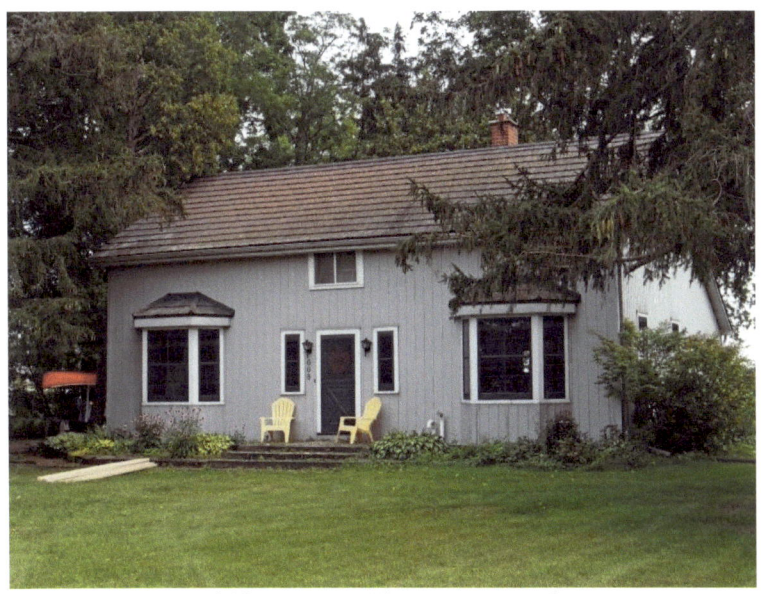

668 Mount Pleasant Road

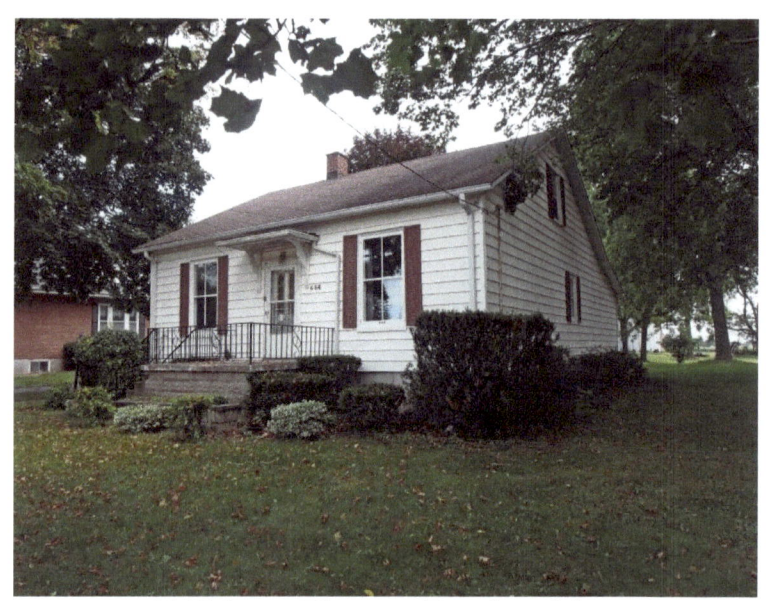

664 Mount Pleasant Road - saltbox

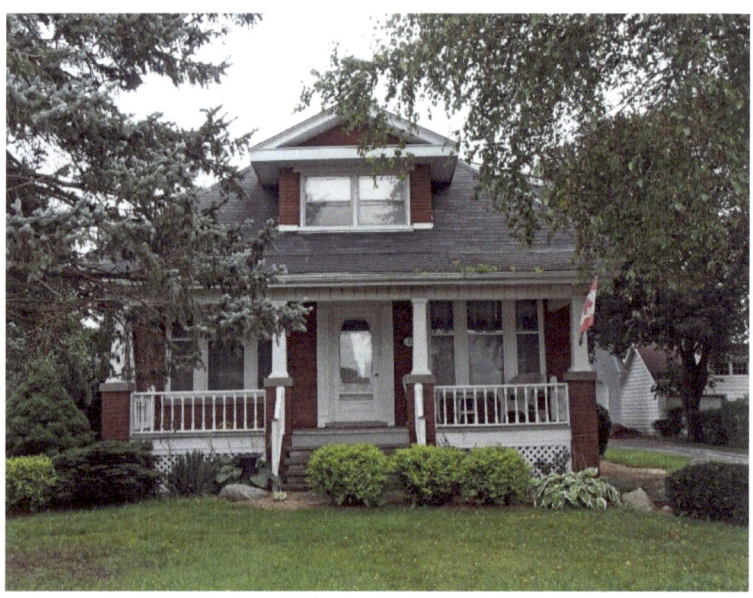

662 Mount Pleasant Road - dormer

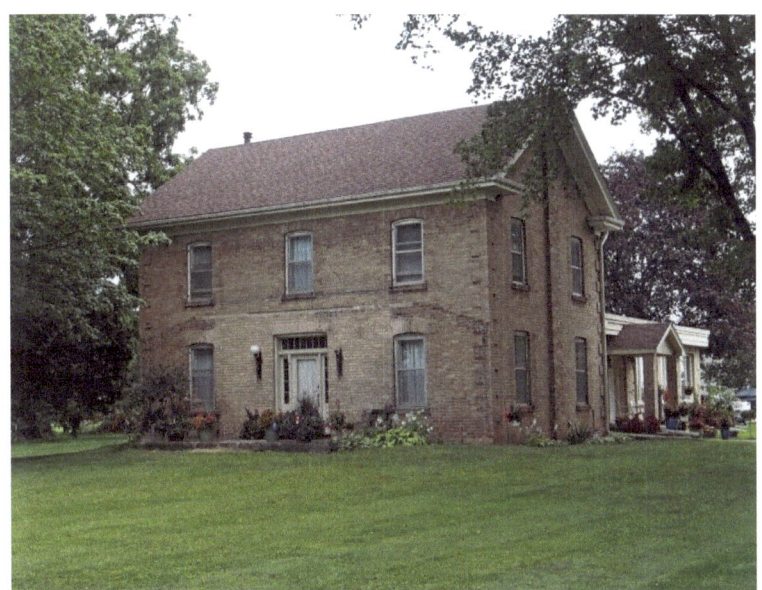

660 Mount Pleasant Road – farmhouse – corner quoins

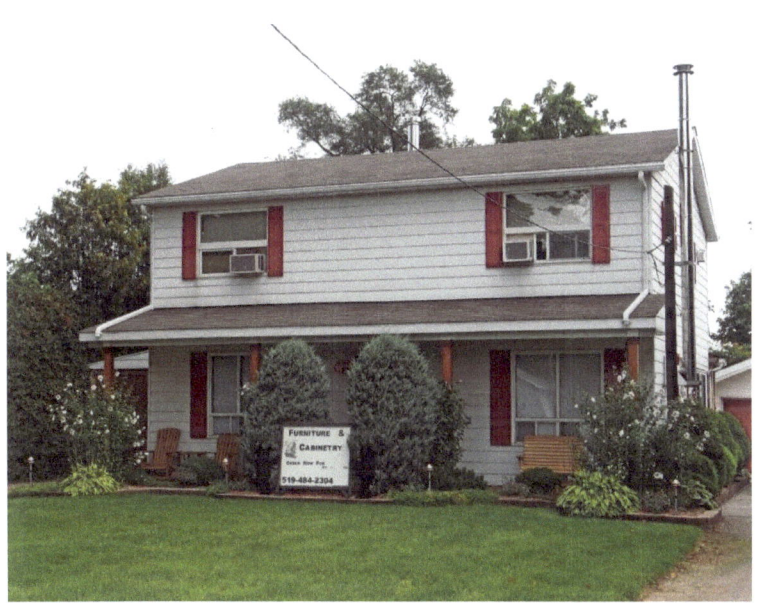

650 Mount Pleasant Road

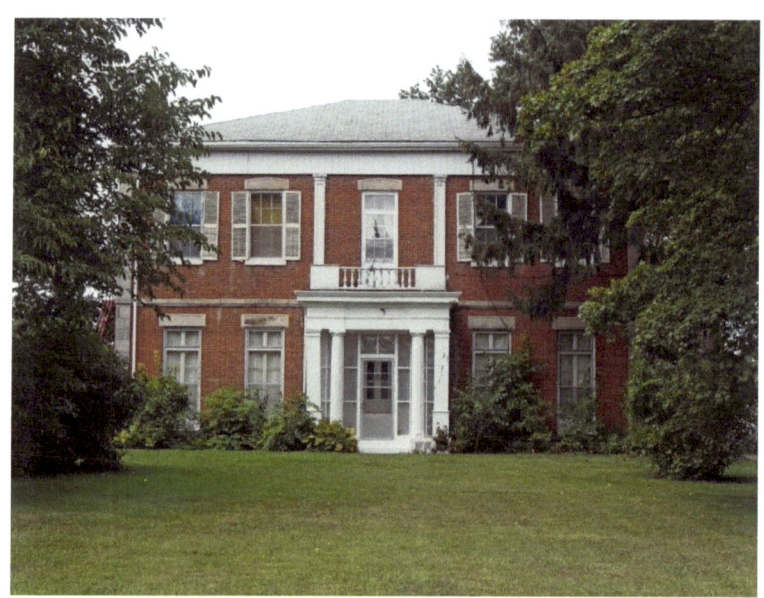

657 Mount Pleasant Road – Abraham Cooke built this Georgian/Greek Revival mansion circa 1840. When Lieutenant Governor of Upper Canada Lord Elgin visited in 1846, he was so impressed he asked for the privilege of naming it "Brucefield" after his family.

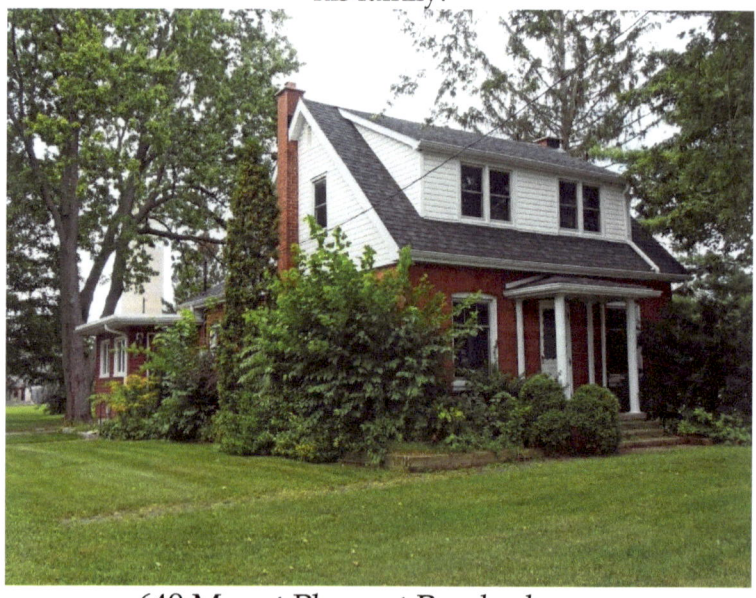

649 Mount Pleasant Road - dormer

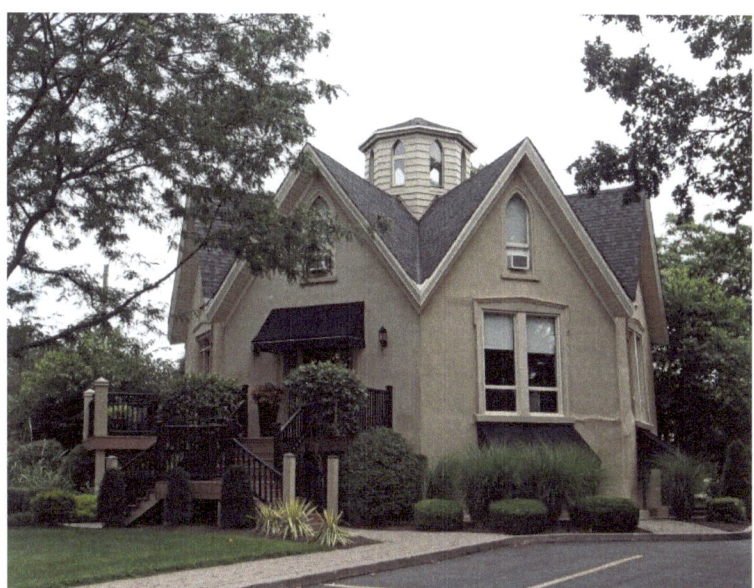

646 Mount Pleasant Road – Scape Spa – This circa 1850 Neo-Gothic style octagon is the only survivor of three similar buildings in Mount Pleasant. Shoemaker Richard Tennant took eight years to build it. Belvedere on the roof.

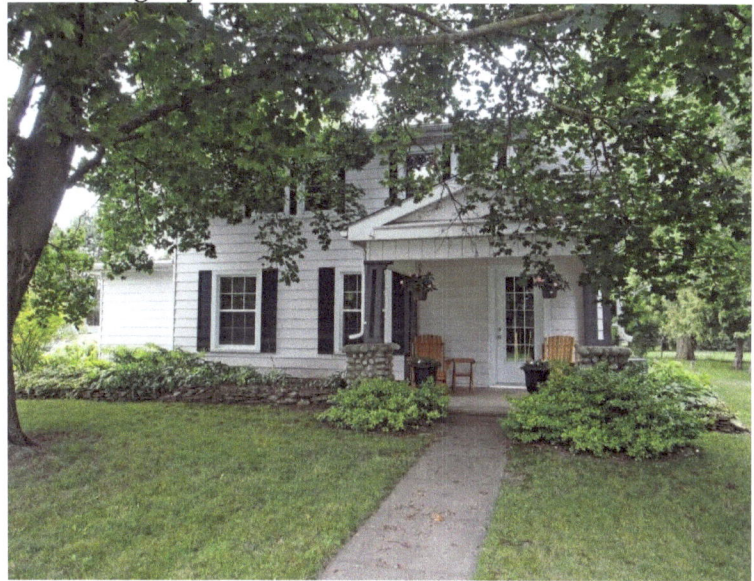

645 Mount Pleasant Road - pediment

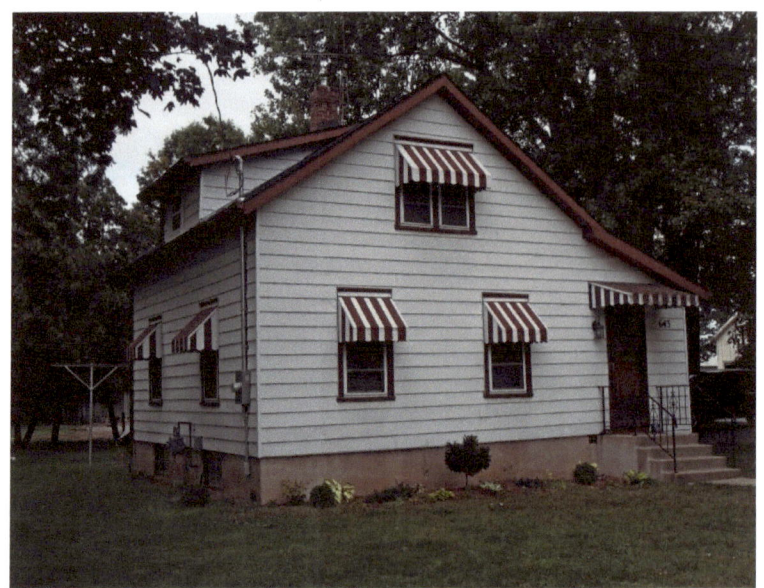

643 Mount Pleasant Road – saltbox, dormer

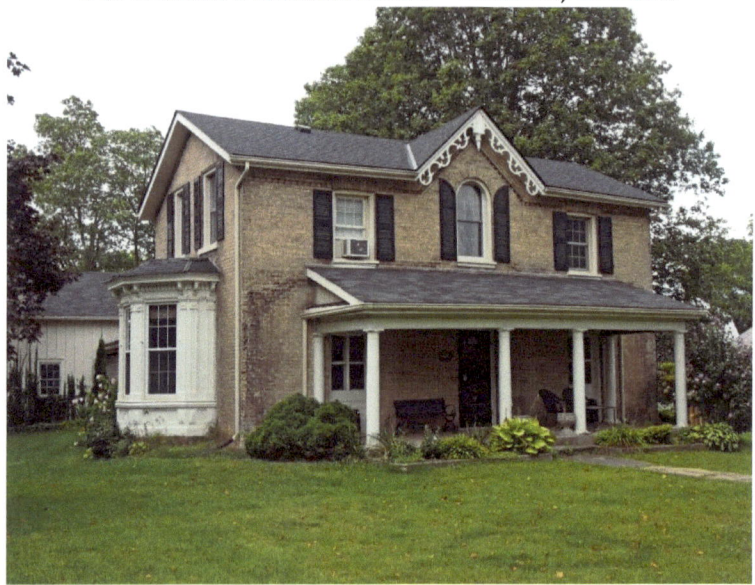

641 Mount Pleasant Road – This farmhouse was built in 1860 in distinctive Regency style evident in the long front windows in fitted panels. The bay window has Victorian details. Both the Phelps and McAllister families have a multi-generation history in the village reaching back to the early 1800s.

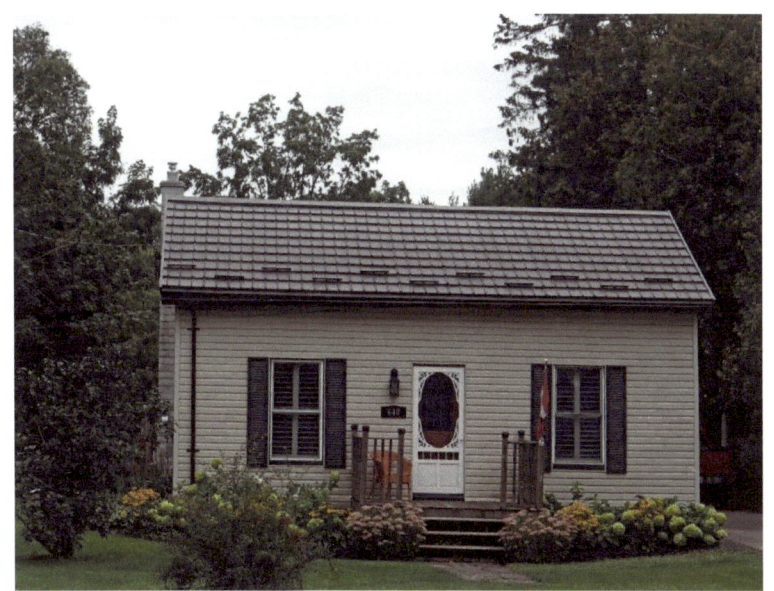

640 Mount Pleasant Road

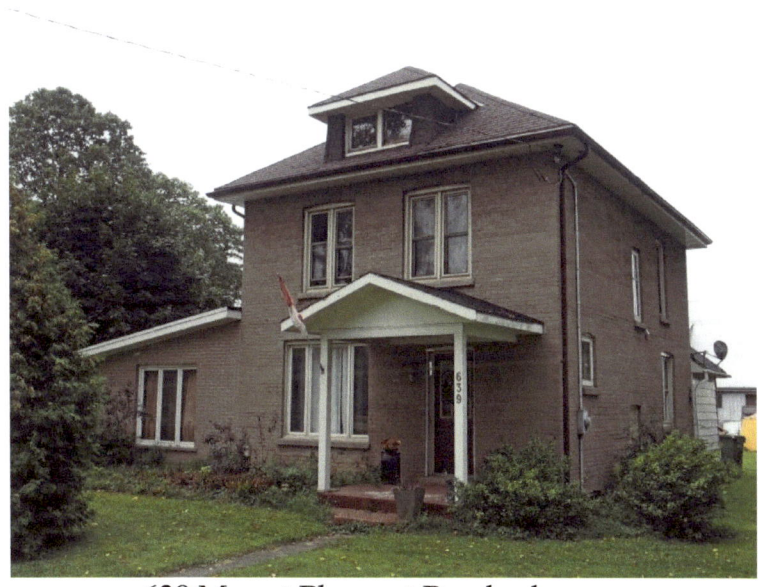

639 Mount Pleasant Road - dormer

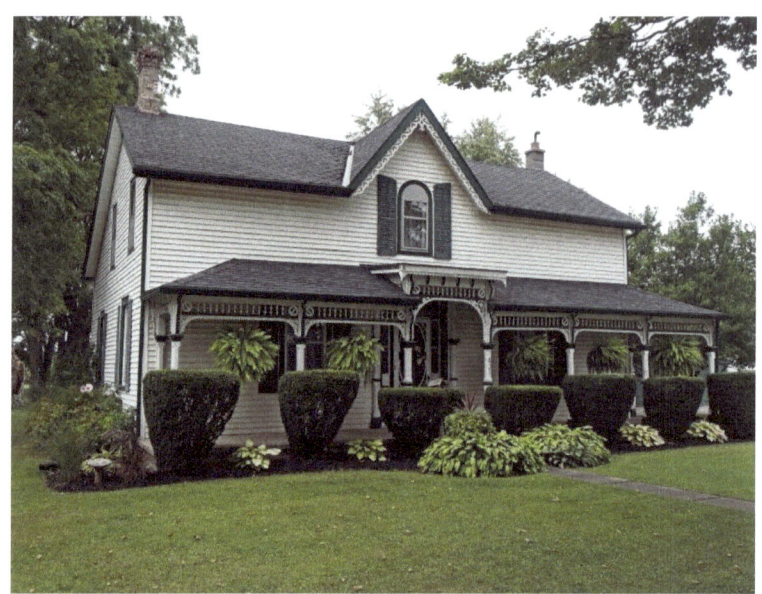

637 Mount Pleasant Road – Emily Townsend House, circa 1860s – Alvah Townsend built this house for his daughter. It is a Neo-Gothic style home which has been well maintained.

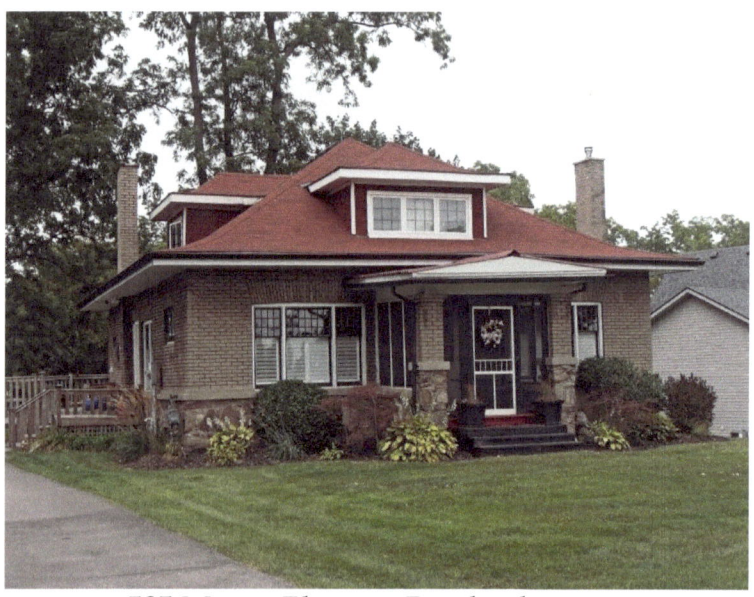

595 Mount Pleasant Road – dormers

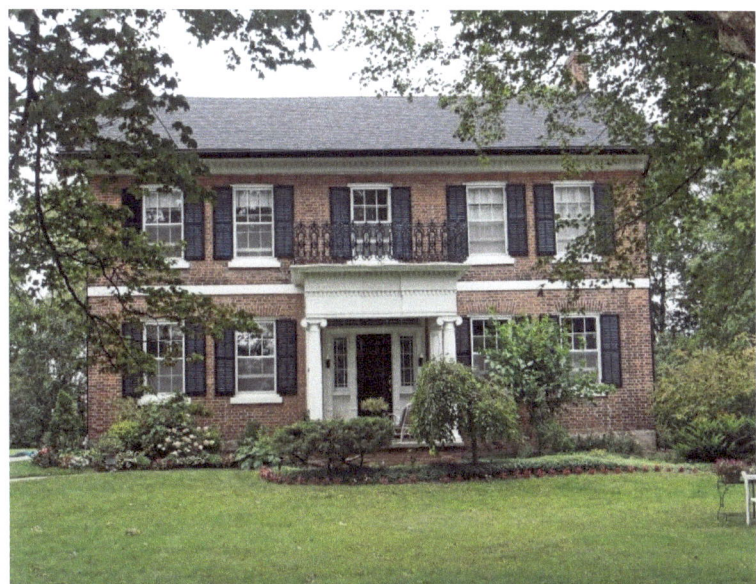

597 Mount Pleasant Road – Georgian Revival built circa 1848 for landowner and carriage maker Alvah Townsend. The style exhibits the horizontal profile and symmetrical arrangement of doors and windows.

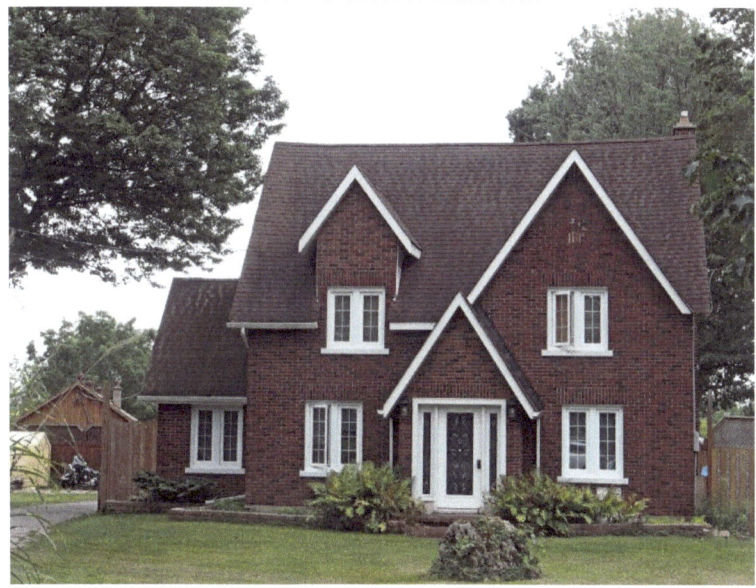

572 Mount Pleasant Road - Vernacular

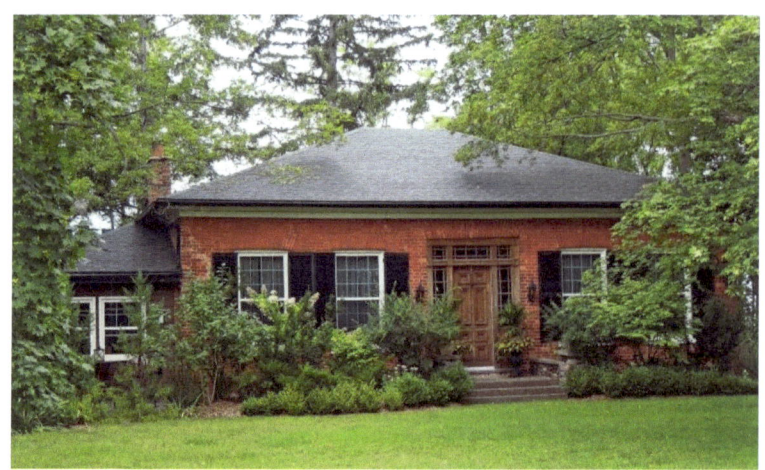

571 Mount Pleasant Road – Biggar Home, 1825 – This split-level, hip-roofed classic Ontario Regency cottage is believed to be one of the oldest homes in The County of Brant. Herbert Biggar, the original owner of the house, was the first M.P.P. for Brant South in 1854.

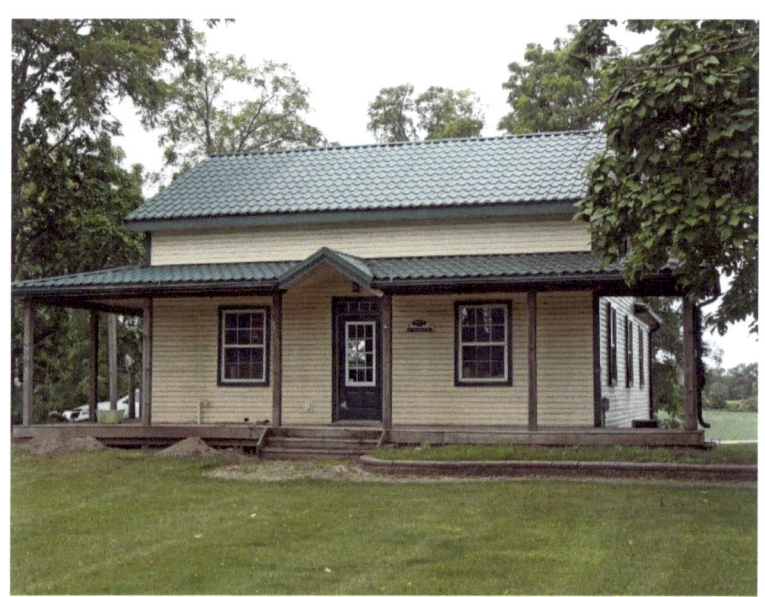

555 Mount Pleasant Road

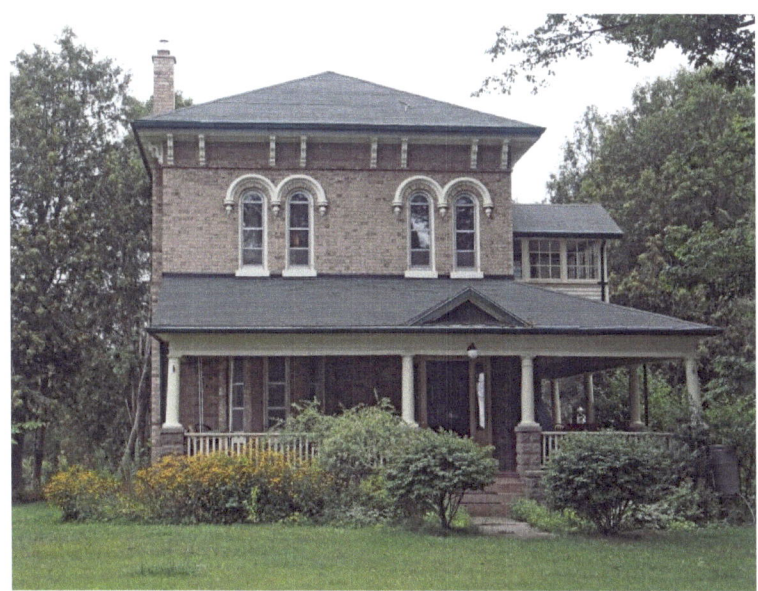

538 Mount Pleasant Road – The Phelps-Guest House, circa 1840s, was built in three stages. The original home was of stone construction with a board and batten addition to the rear and a buff brick Italianate addition added to the front in the 1880s.

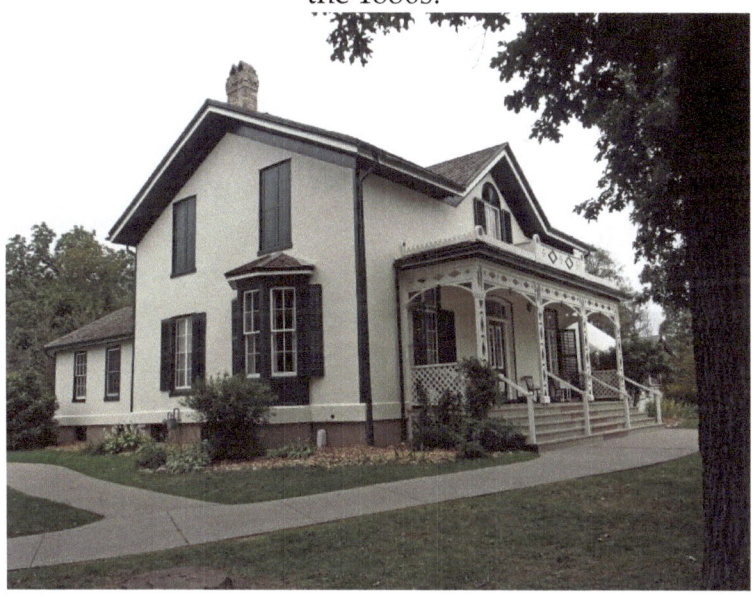

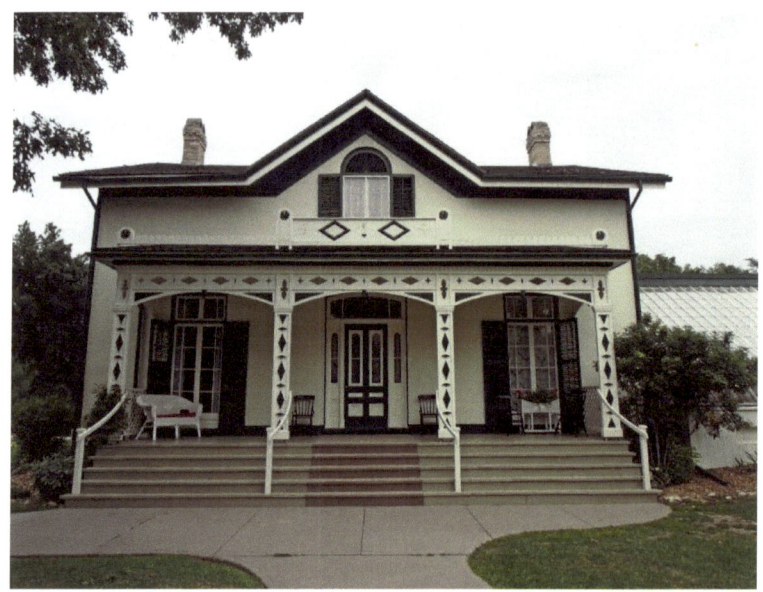

94 Tutela Heights Road – The Bell Homestead was built in 1858 by the original owner and builder Robert Morton. It was here on July 26, 1874 during his summer vacation that Alexander Graham Bell discovered the fundamental concept for the telephone. He returned to Brantford from Boston, Massachusetts in September 1875 at which time he drafted the patent specifications for the device. In 1876 Bell set up and completed the world's first long distance telephone call between Brantford and Paris.

The homestead evokes the formative influence of Bell's father, an authority on the acoustics of speech, and of his mother who was deaf. They stimulated their son's lifelong interest in teaching the deaf to speak, a passion that proved crucial to the discovery of the telephone.

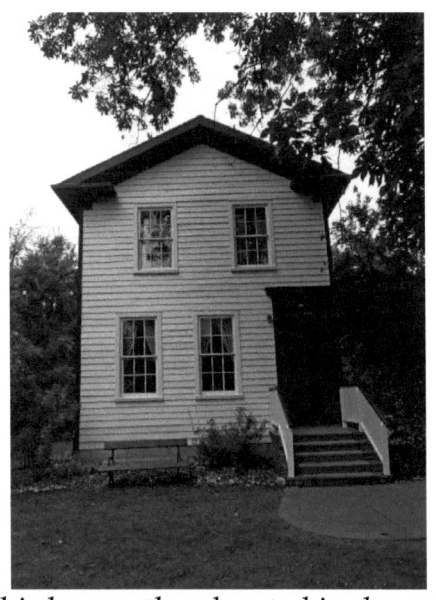

In 1877 this house, then located in downtown Brantford, became Canada's First Telephone Business Office. It was the residence of Reverend Thomas Philip Henderson (1816-1887), a former Baptist minister and school inspector in Paris, Ontario, who had in 1870 encouraged the Bell family to come to Brantford. In 1877 he retired from the ministry to become the first General Agent for the telephone business in Canada and played a significant role in its establishment and development. Henderson used this house as his office until 1880 when he joined the newly formed Bell Canada in Montreal as Purchasing Agent and Storekeeper.

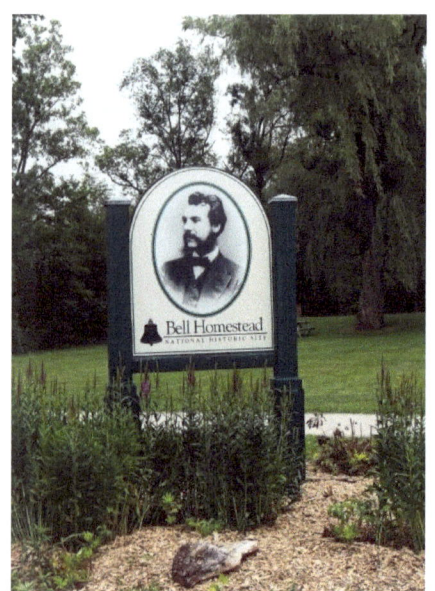 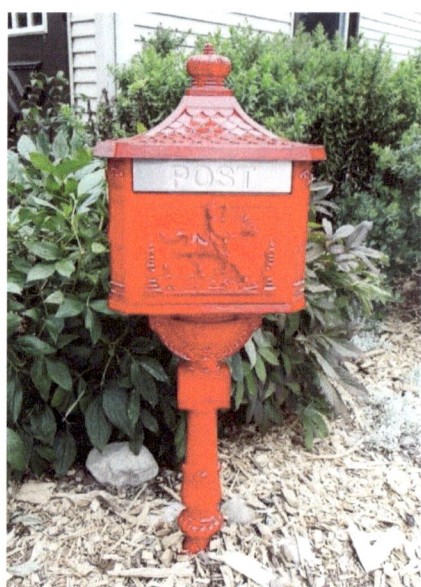

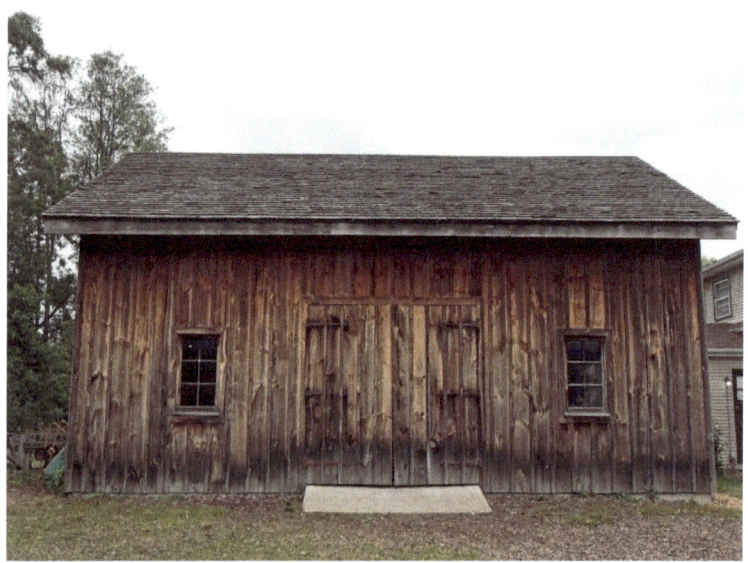
94 Tutela Heights Road barn

# Newport

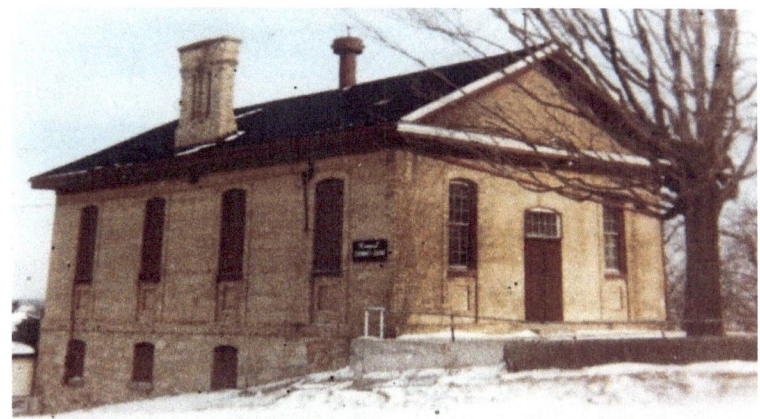

The brick Newport School Section No. 10 school house was built in 1872. It closed in 1964 and was converted to a community centre. Due to instability of the river bank, the building was demolished in 2007.

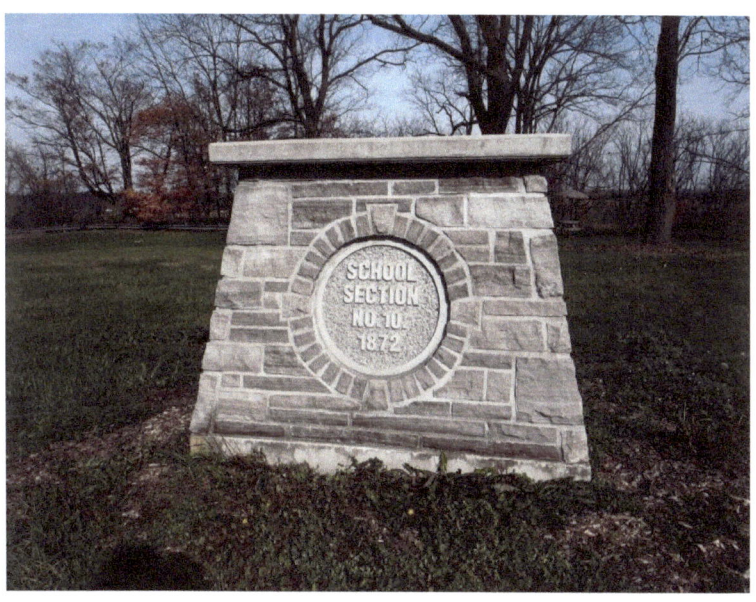

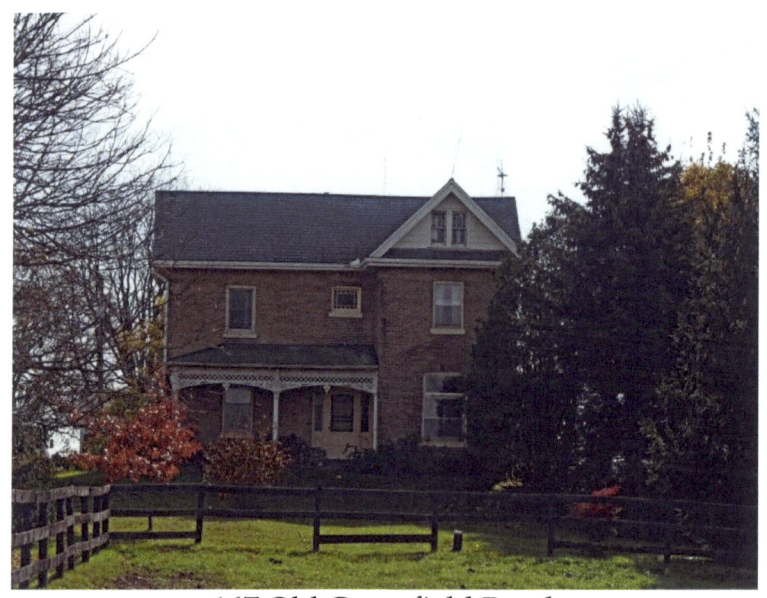
167 Old Greenfield Road

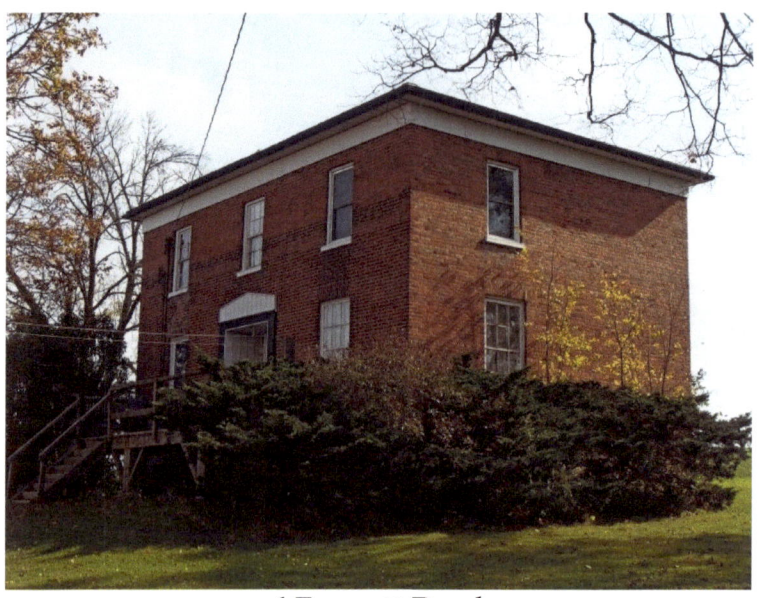
6 Fawcett Road

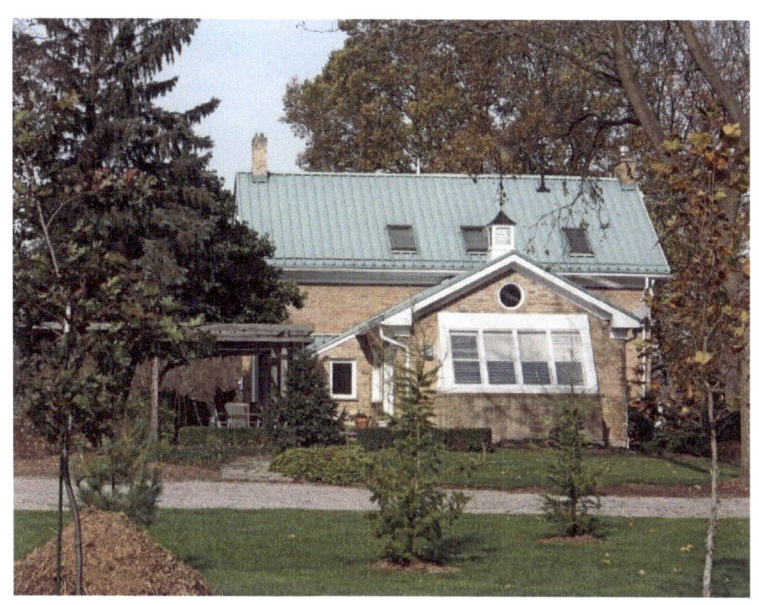

182 River Road

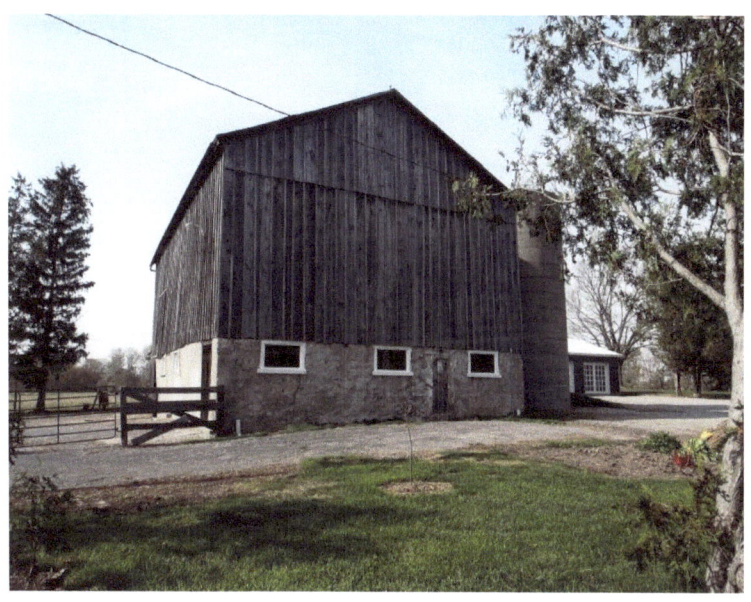

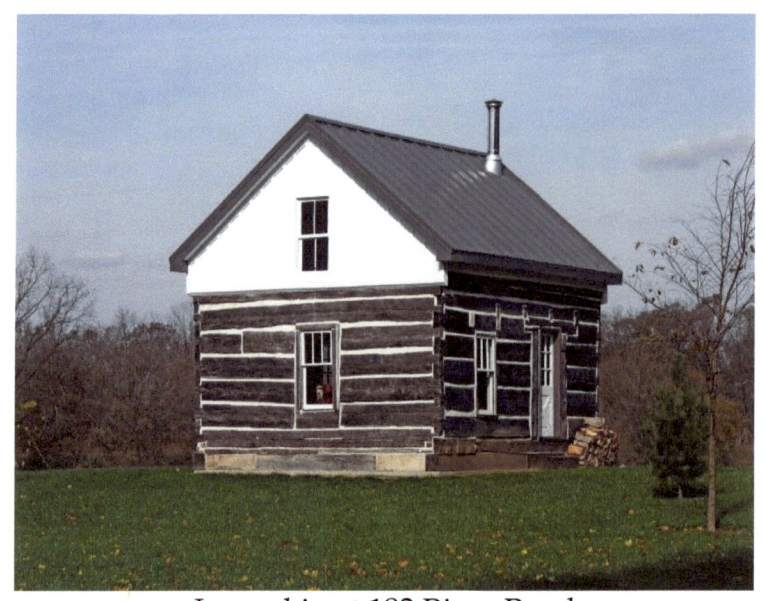

Log cabin at 182 River Road

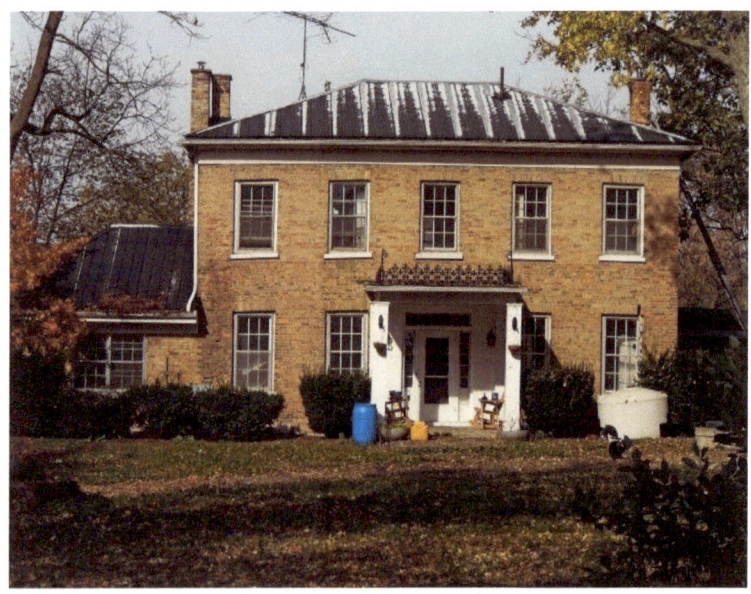

190 River Road

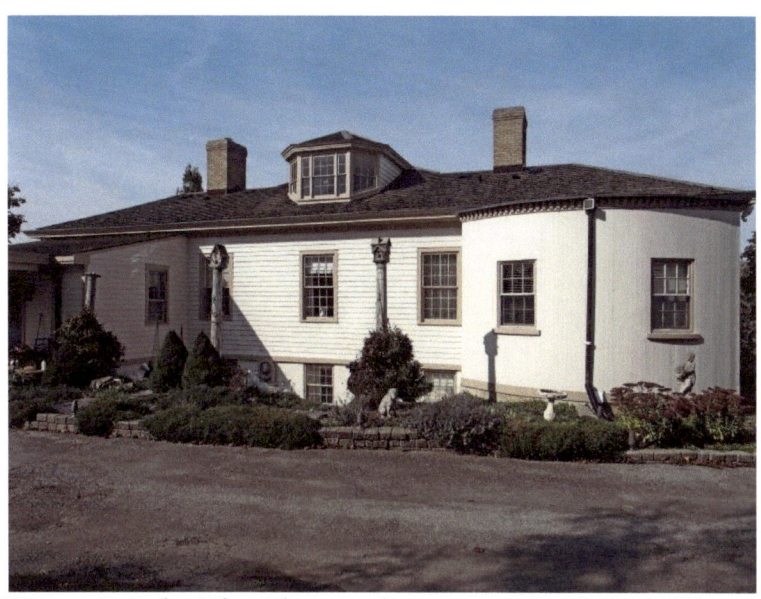

255 River Road – The Thomas house was built in 1835 at 1030 Colborne Street East by Captain Joseph Thomas on land purchased by his father John Thomas who helped build the Mohawk Chapel. John was a close friend of Captain Joseph Brant. The walls are one foot thick and the double-stud main frame is made of 12″ x 12″ beams. Massive fireplaces were built up from the lower level indicating that the masons did this work before the framers began. In 1993, to make way for development on Colborne Street, the house was cut in half and moved to where it sits today on top of the small hill on River Road. The owner has lovingly been restoring this home to its former glory.

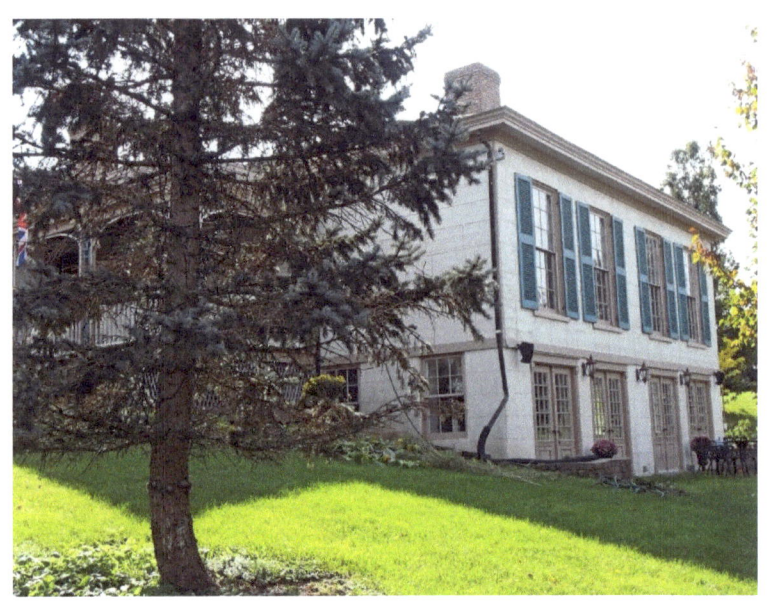

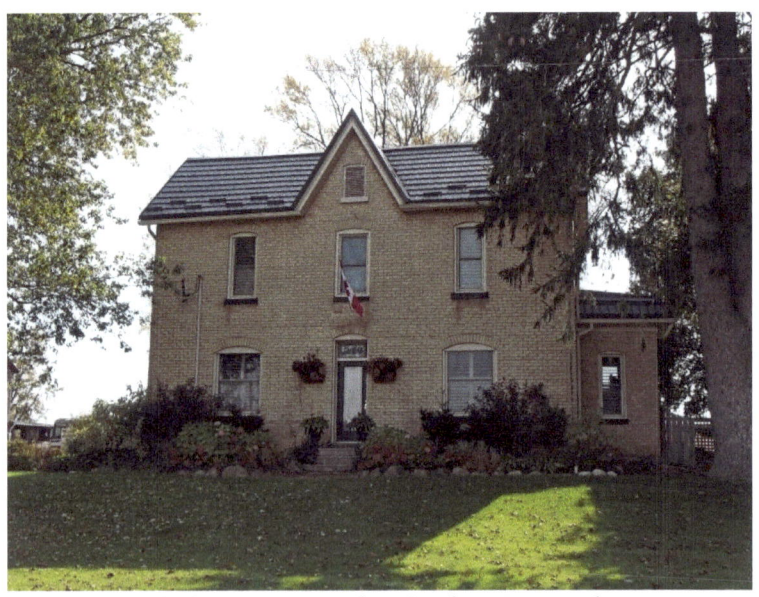

219 River Road – Gothic Revival

# Onondaga

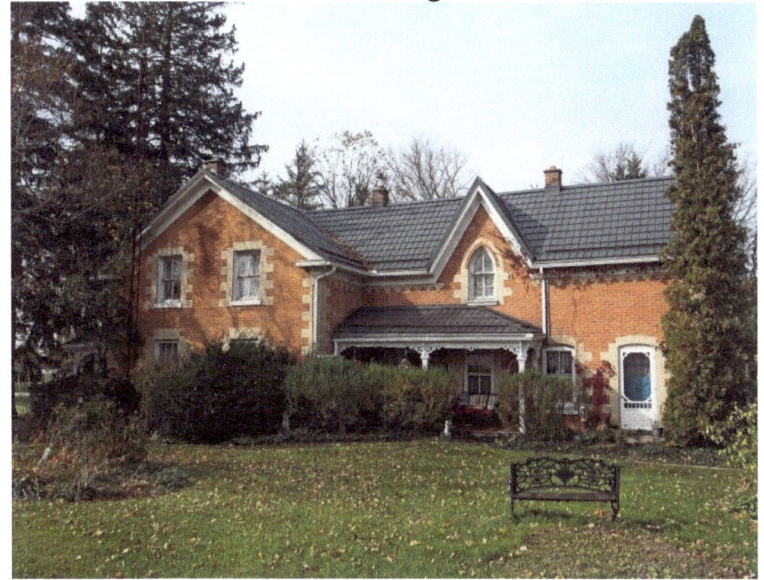

744 Highway 54

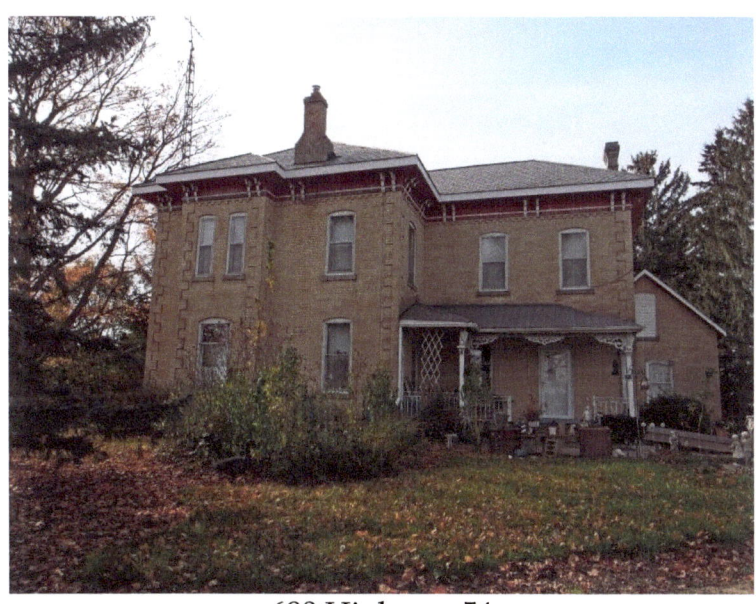

690 Highway 54

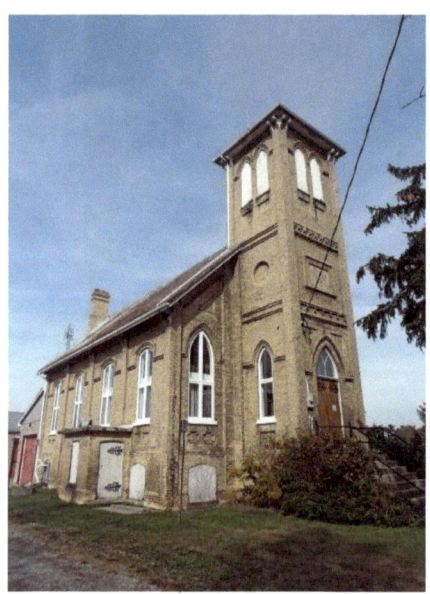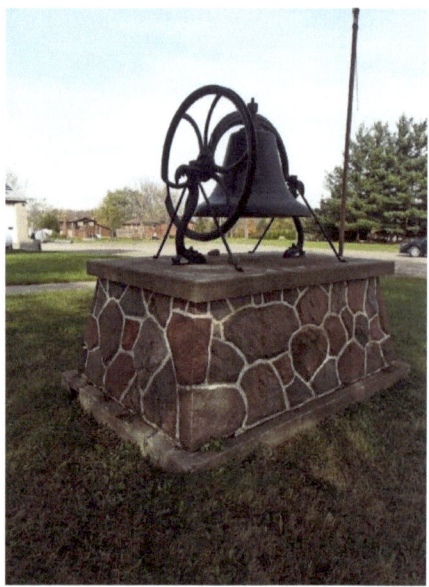

734 Highway 54 – This building was originally School Section #5, Onondaga. In 1975, the Onondaga Municipal Office was set up here. Presently, the County of Brant Service Area Office and the Onondaga Fire Department are housed here. In front of the Service Area Office is a cairn celebrating the six school sections. A school bell from one of the rural schools sits appropriately on top of the cairn.

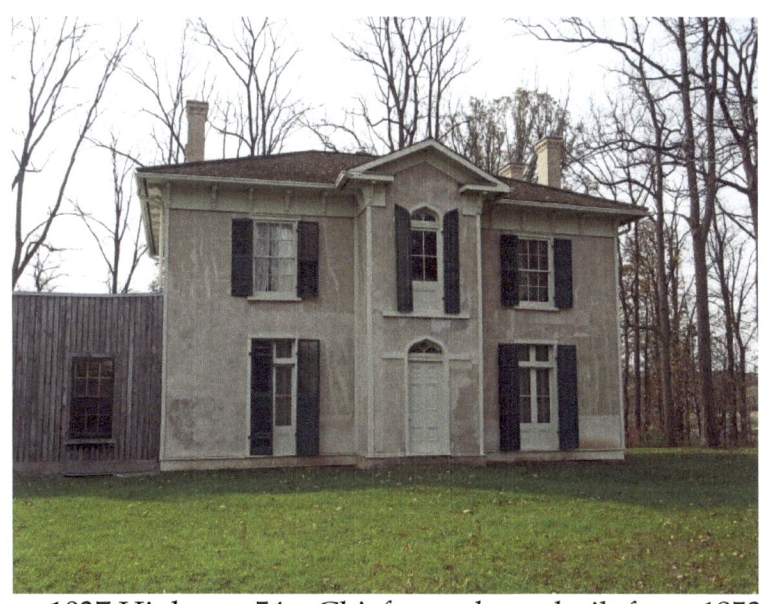

1037 Highway 54 – Chiefswood was built from 1853-1856 by Chief George Johnson for his English wife Emily Howells. The two cultural traditions were blended in the construction of the house in the Italianate style. It has two front doors – one facing the Grand River and the other the highway. The large two-storey mansion is symmetrical with matching French windows. One of George and Emily's children was Emily Pauline Johnson, the famous Indian poetess. Among her works are: "The Song My Paddle Sings" and "Train Dogs."

Check them out at http://www.bartleby.com/246/1267.html
https://www.poemhunter.com/poem/the-train-dogs/

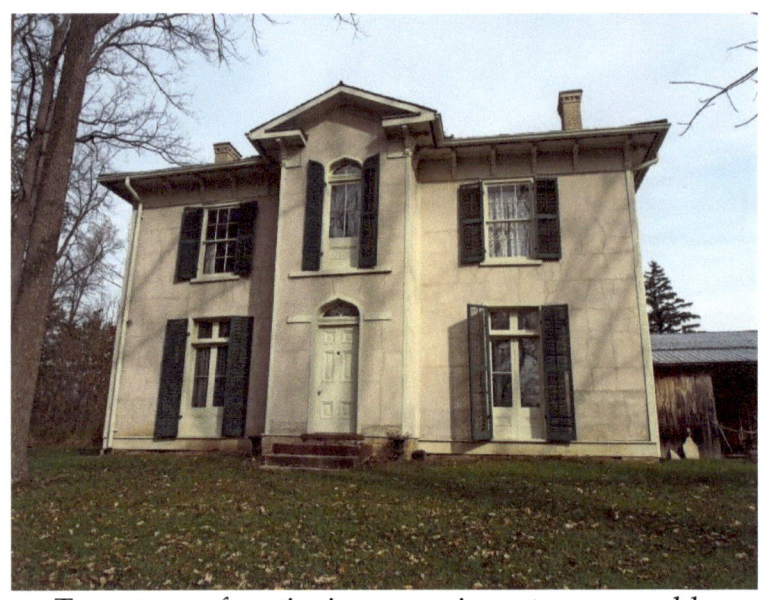

Two-storey frontispiece, cornice return on gable

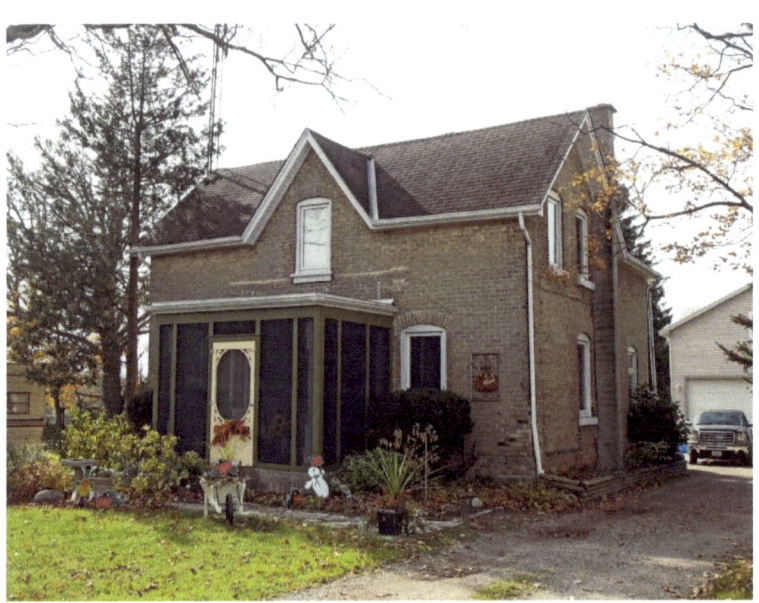

Tuscarora Street - Gothic

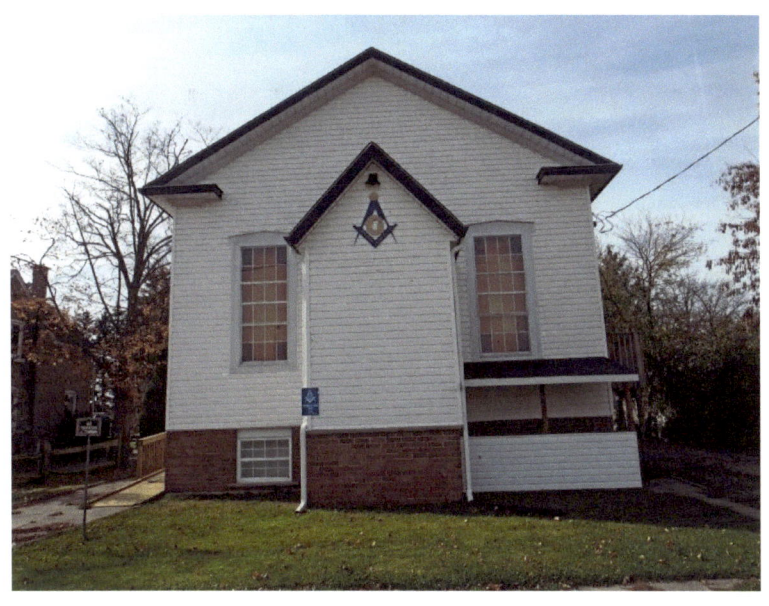

Tuscarora Street – cornice return on gable

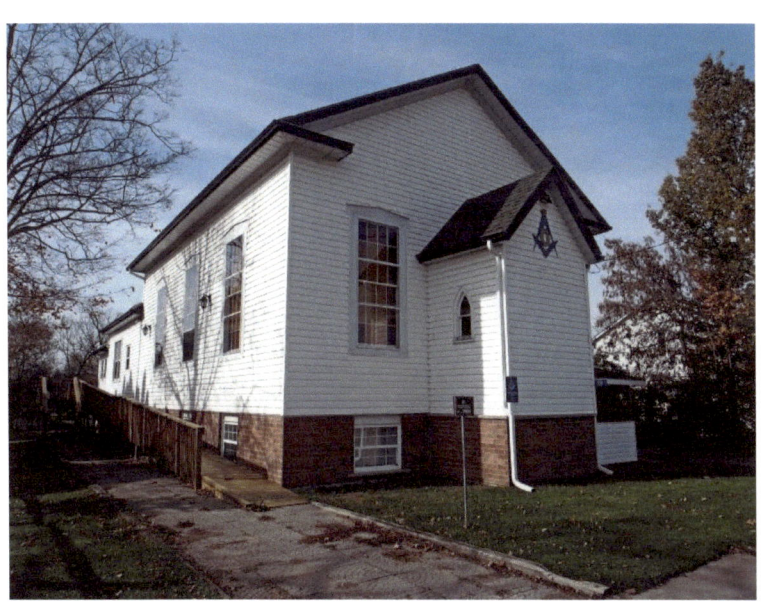

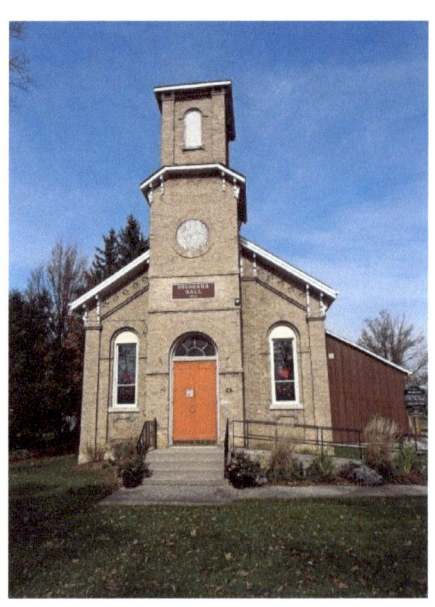

42 Brantford Street – Onondaga Hall – 1874 – Neo-Gothic – white brick, three-storey tower, cornice brackets, transom window above door

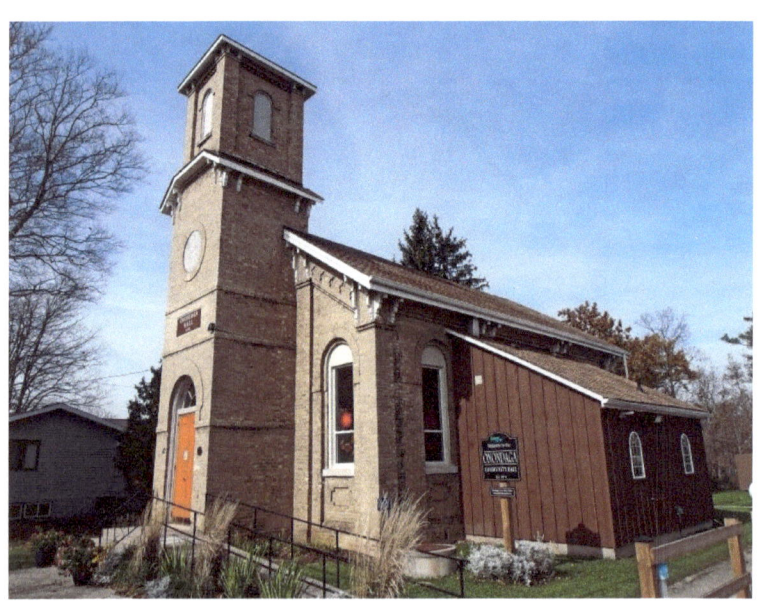

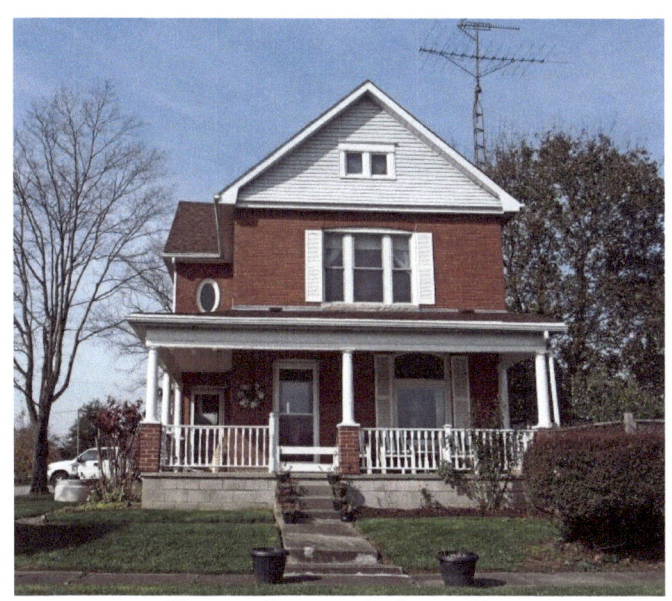

Centre Street - Edwardian

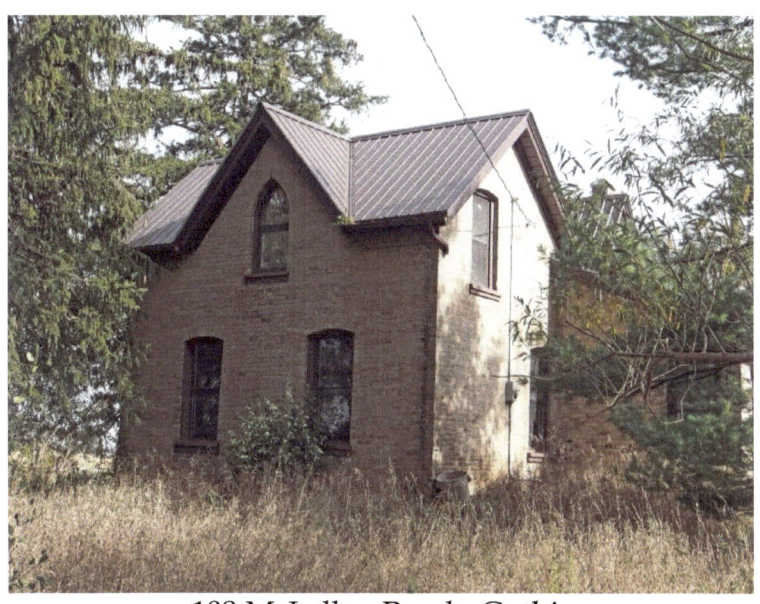

108 McLellan Road - Gothic

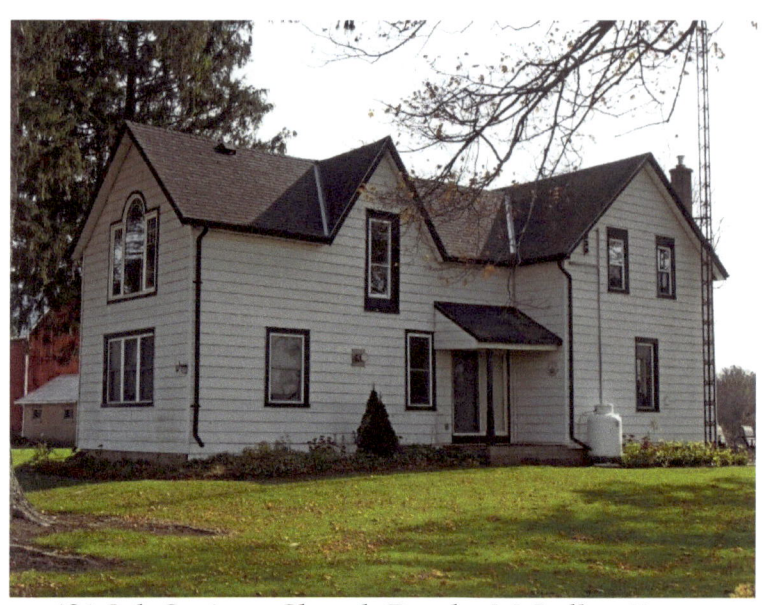

421 Salt Springs Church Road – McLellan Farms

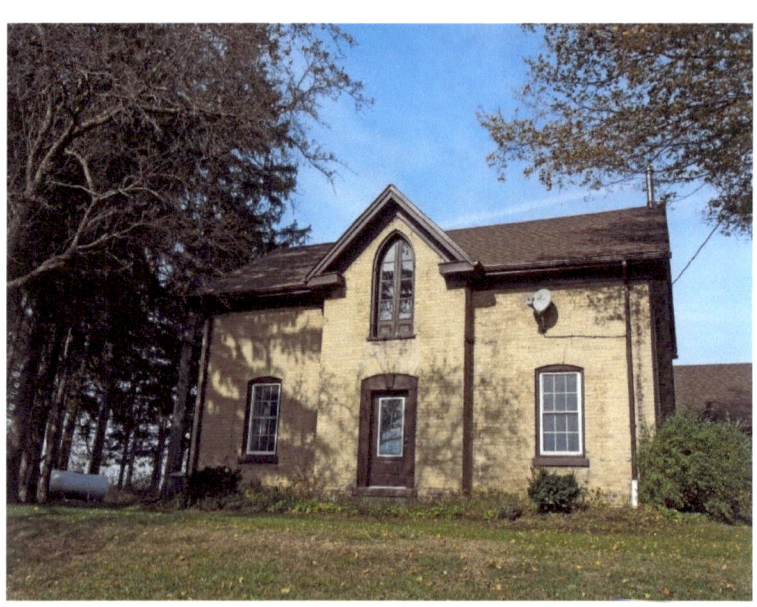

360 Salt Springs Church Road – circa 1880 – white brick

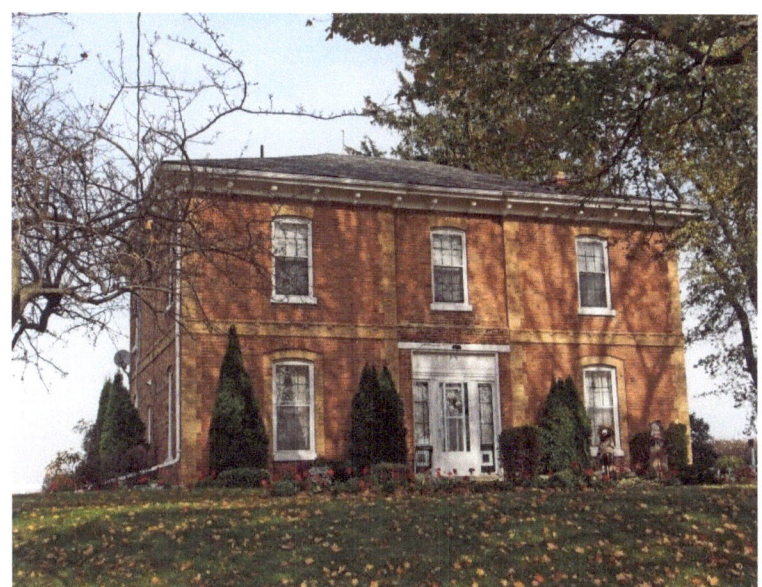

382 Salt Springs Church Road – circa 1835 – The house has buff brick quoins and decorative brickwork, with recessed brickwork around the front windows. It was built for Judge James Hamilton (McNaughton) and has been in the Hamilton family for five generations. The brick used for the house was manufactured on the site.

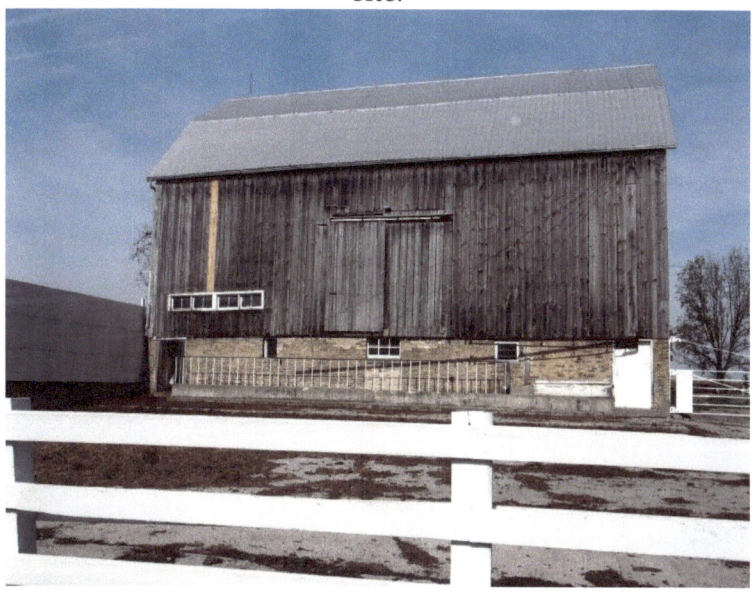

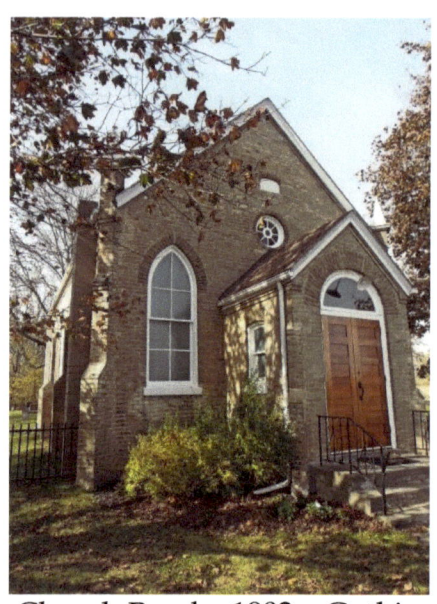

61 Salt Springs Church Road – 1902 – Gothic – The road and church were so named because saltwater springs were located near The Grand River Mission. In 1822 the Grand River Mission was established her by Wesleyan Methodists to minister to the Six Nations people.

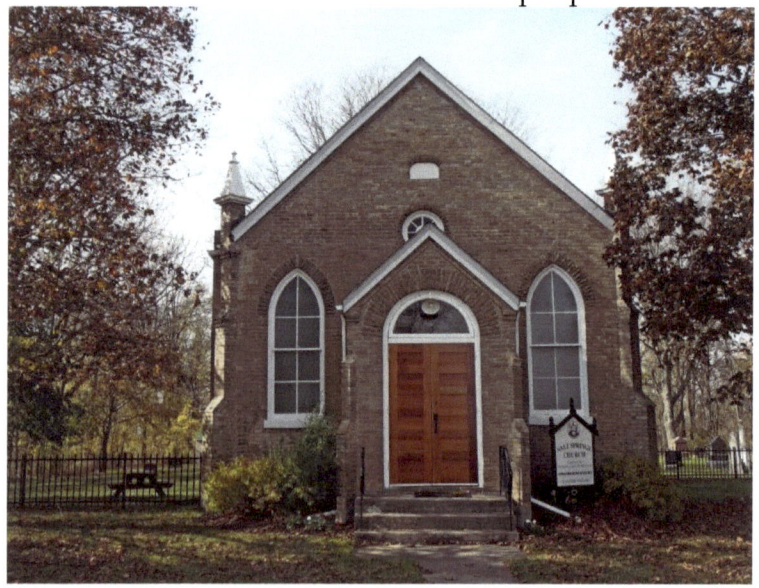

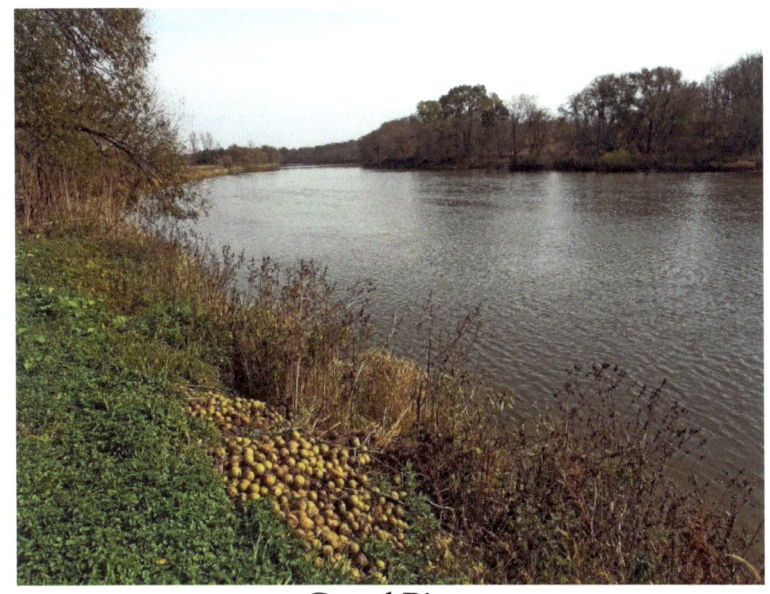

Grand River

## Middleport

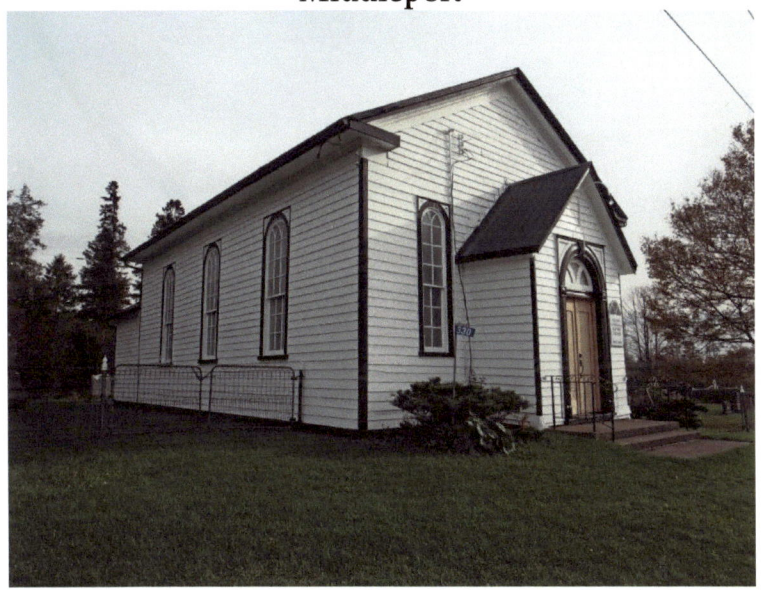

330 Baptist Church Road – 1857 – clapboard-sided church with rounded windows

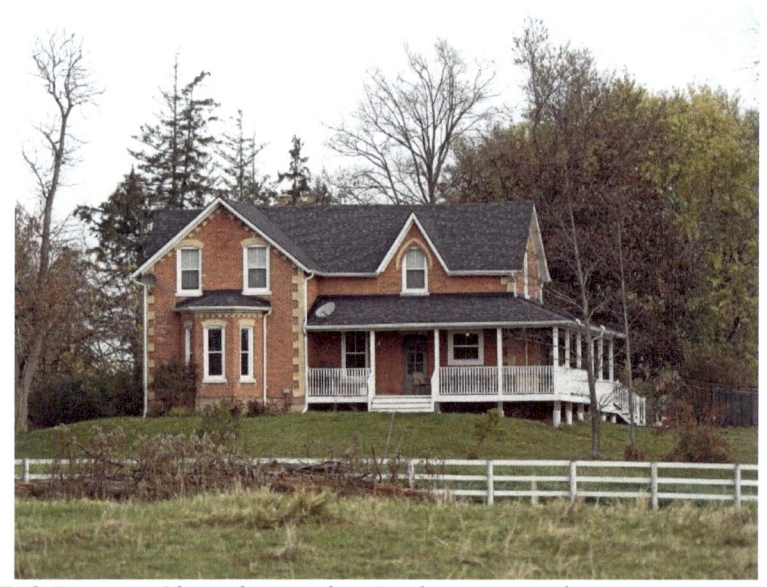
518 Baptist Church Road – Gothic Revival, corner quoins

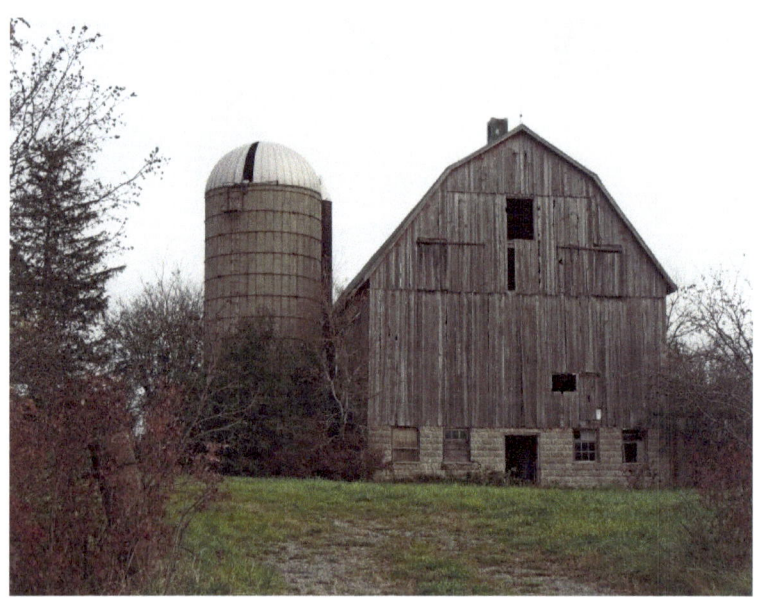

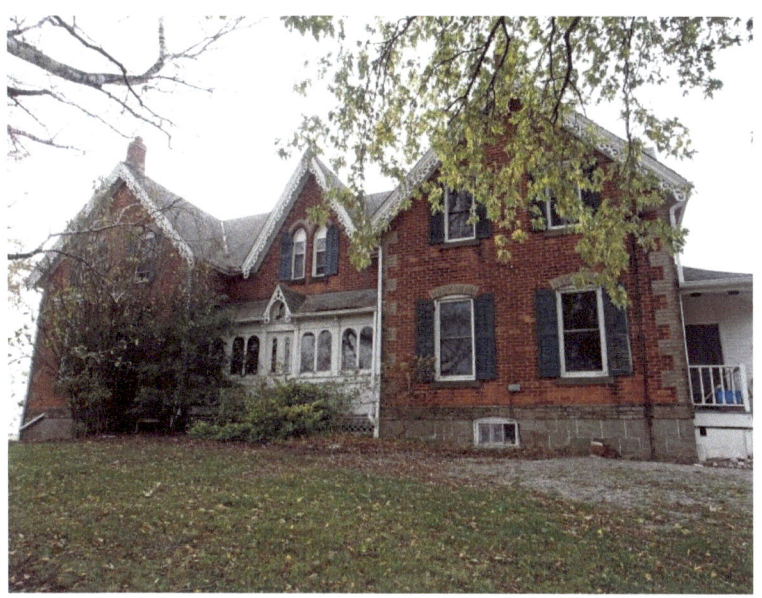

291 Baptist Church Road – Howden Home and Barns, 1883 – In 1856, Thomas Howden and his wife Jane came from Ireland and purchased this 100 acre farm. Their eleven children grew up here. There are 14 rooms, 3 sets of stairs, and more than 50 windows and doors. Three gables trimmed bargeboard contain Gothic windows. The front and side verandas are enclosed with pairs of rounded arched windows and the small gable on the front veranda contains a tiny Gothic window. Quoins accent the corners of the house.

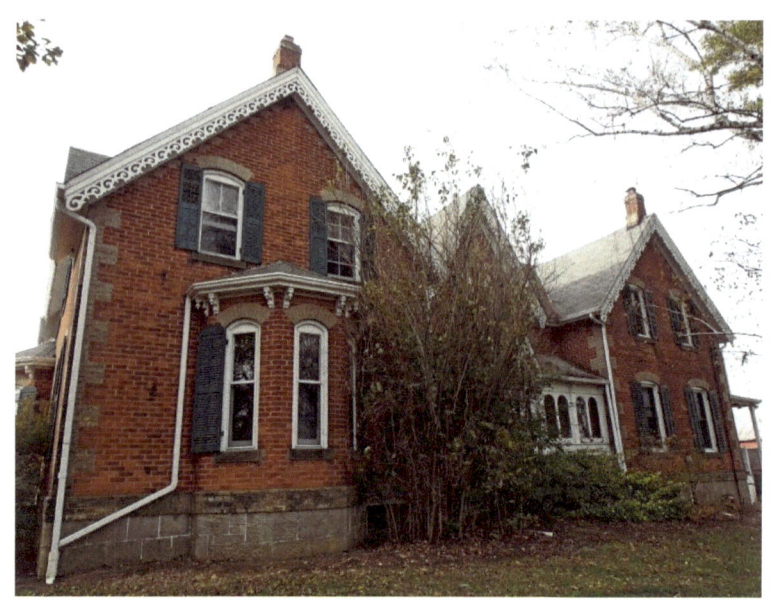

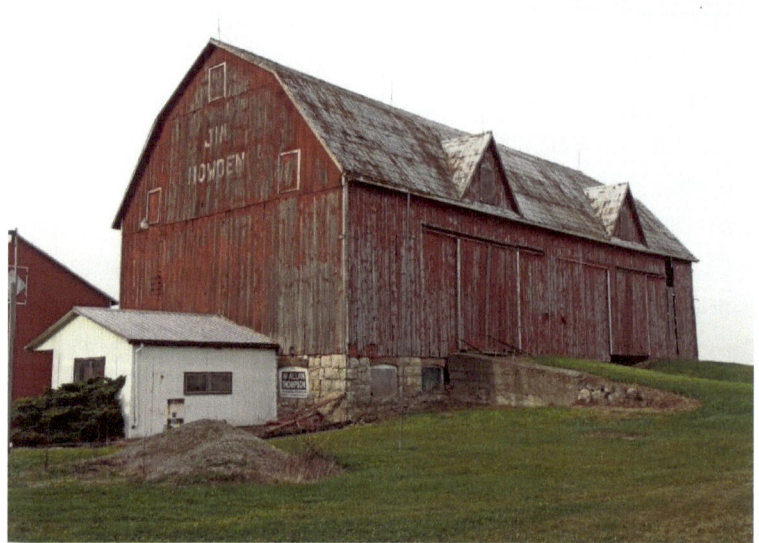

291 Baptist Church Road – an unusual feature on the barn is the dormer over each of the two large doors.

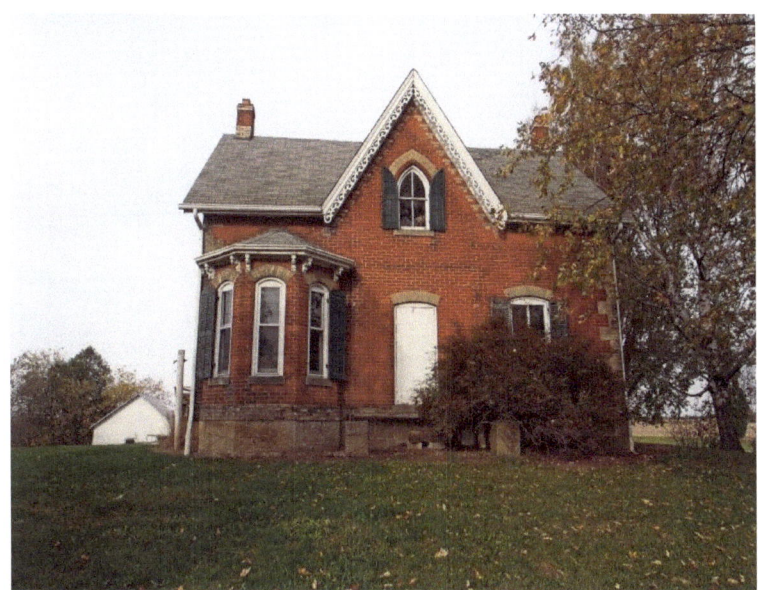

291 Baptist Church Road – Gothic, verge board trim on gable, bay window with cornice brackets

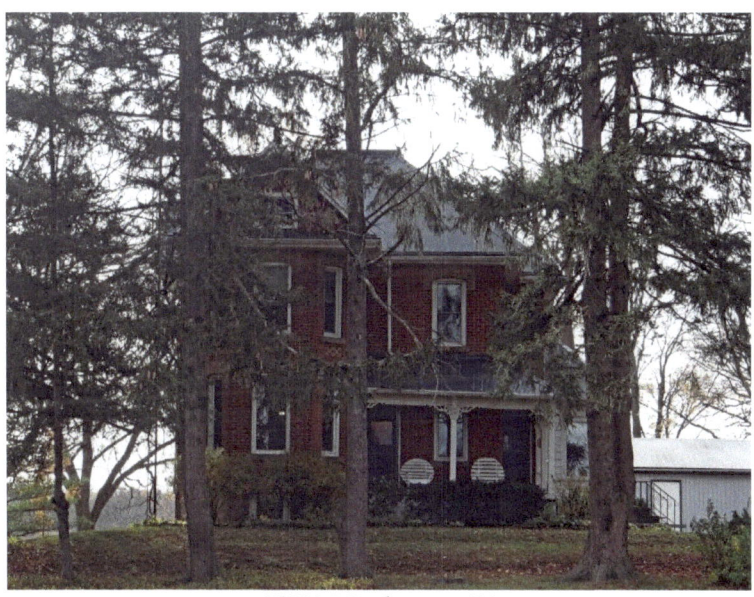

1374 Highway 54

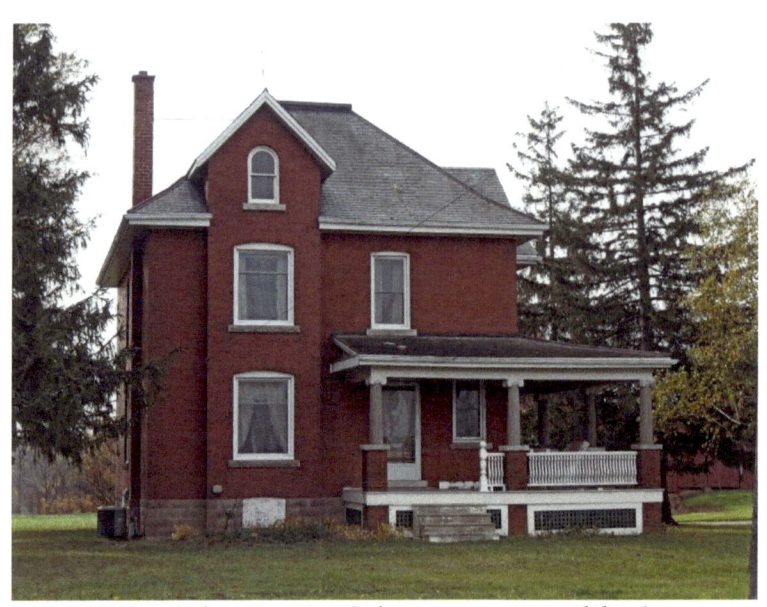

1343 Highway 54 – 2½-storey tower-like bay

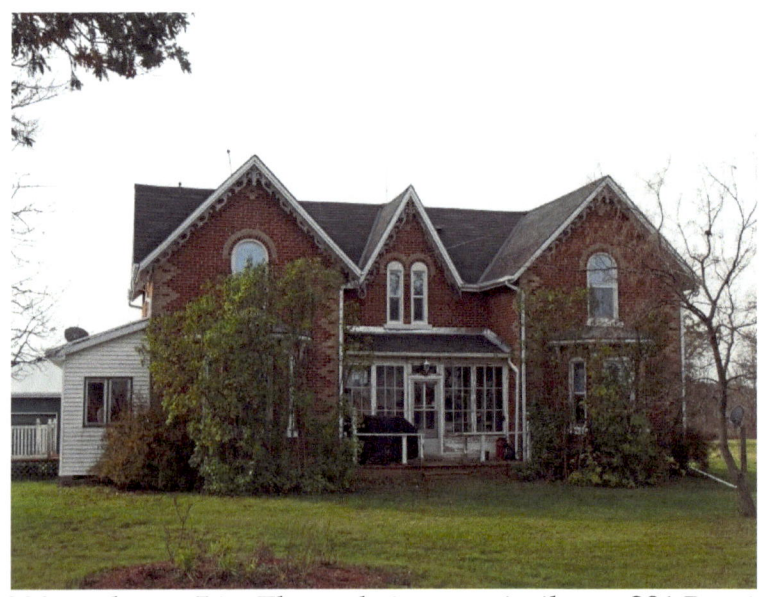

1329 Highway 54 – The style is very similar to 291 Baptist Church Road.

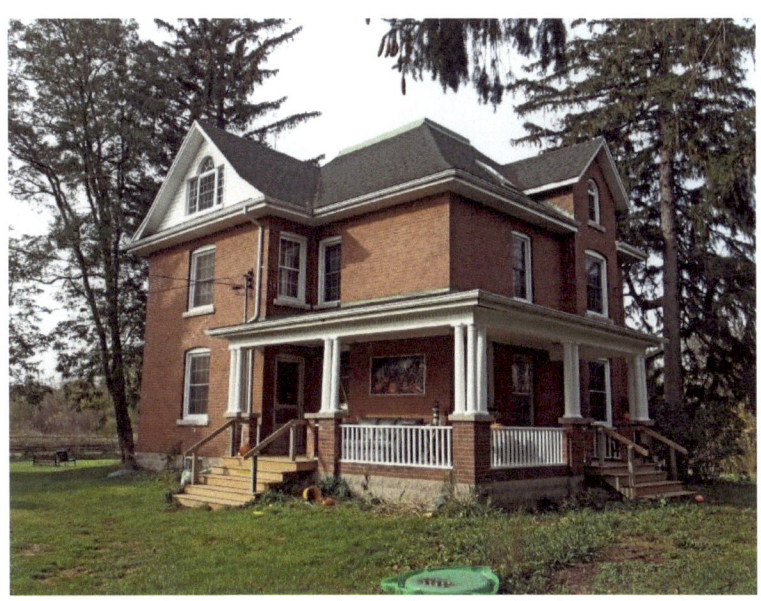

1229 Highway 54 – Edwardian, Palladian window

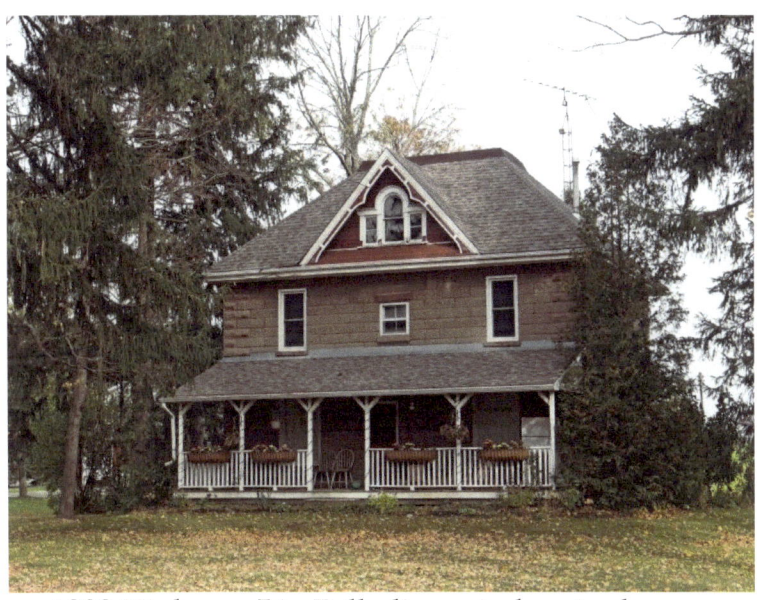

1208 Highway 54 - Palladian window in dormer

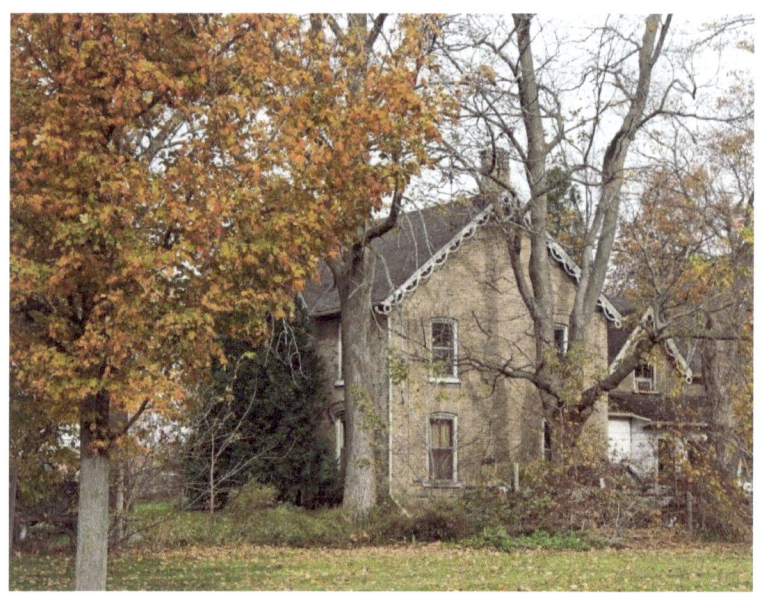

1218 Highway 54 – Gothic – verge board trim on gables, corner quoins

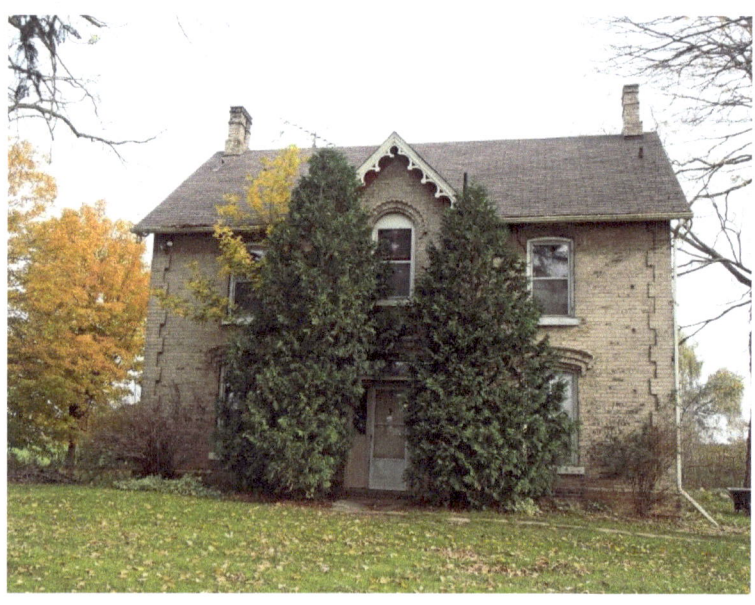

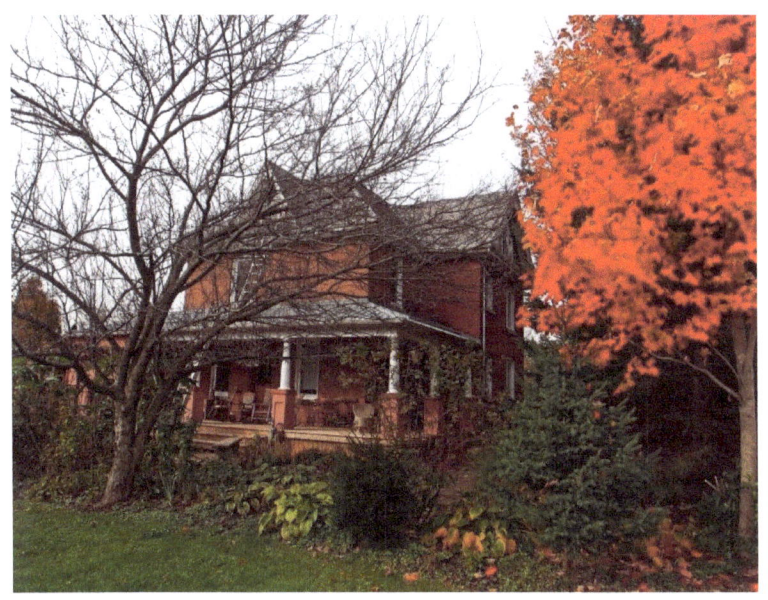

1171 Highway 54 – Edwardian, Palladian window, wraparound veranda

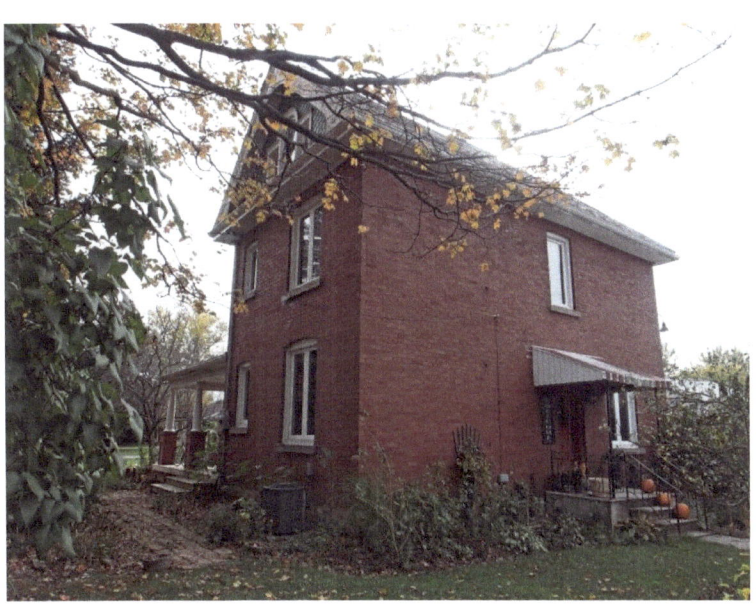

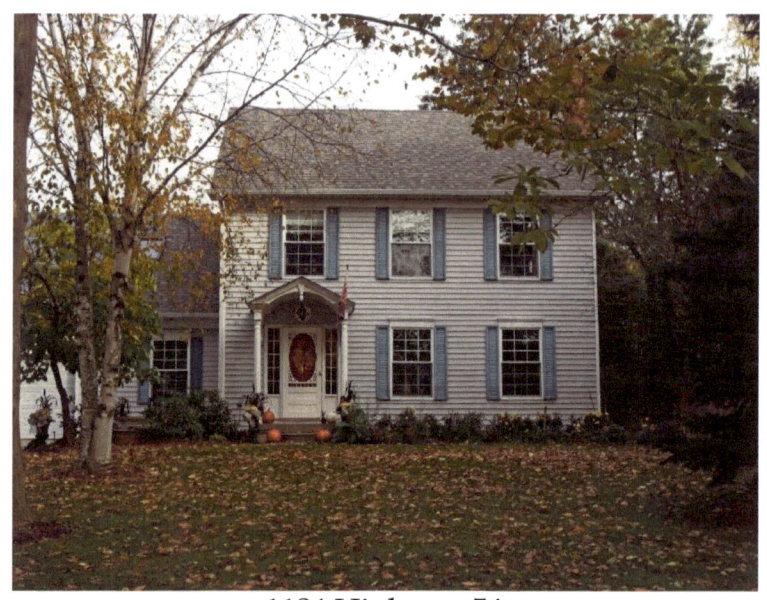

1184 Highway 54

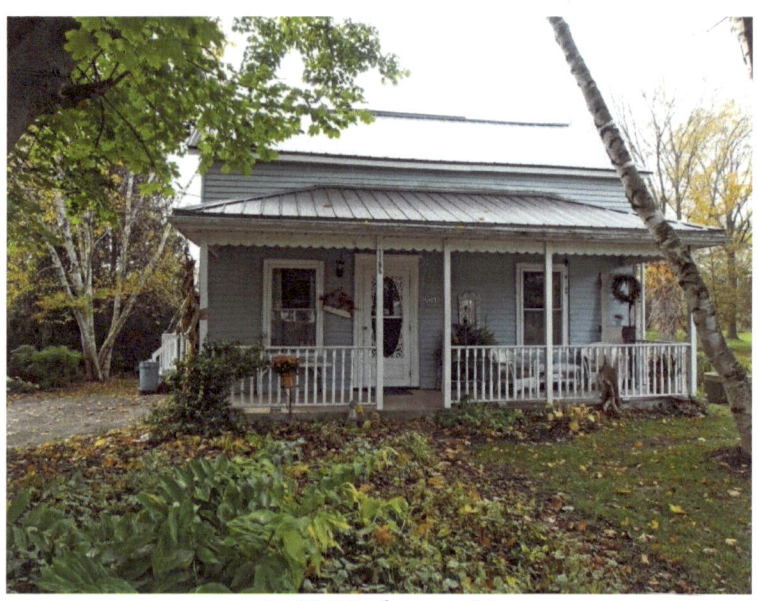

1165 Highway 54

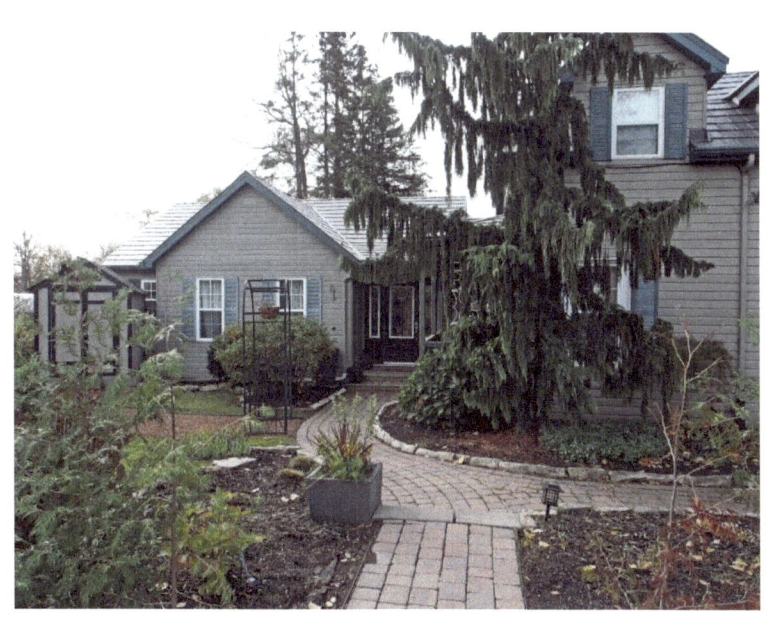

1155 Highway 54 - dormers

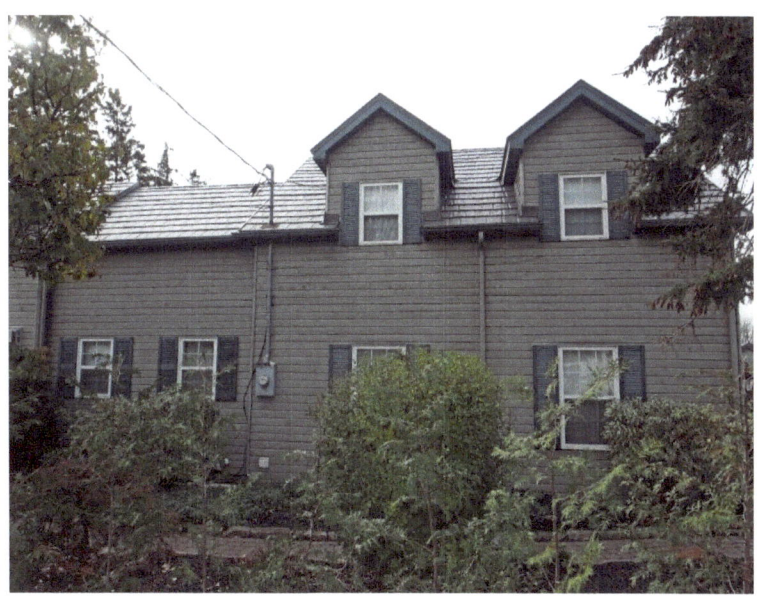

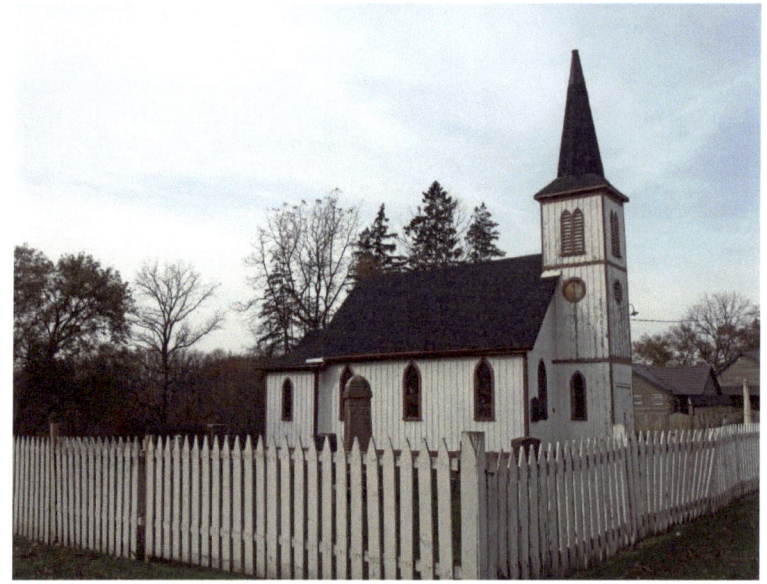

1159 Highway 54 – St. Paul's Anglican Church, 1868 – board and batten, bell tower

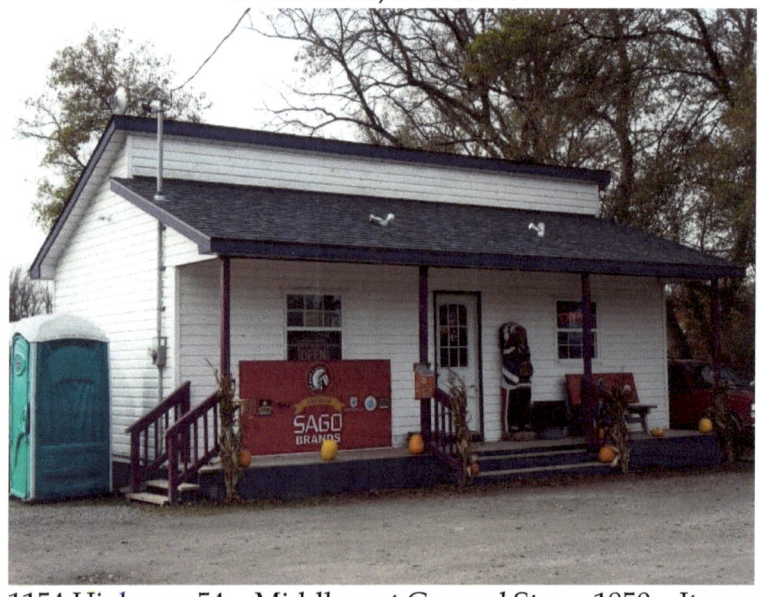

1154 Highway 54 – Middleport General Store, 1850 – It was constructed with wide pine boards about one-inch thick that were laid horizontally end to end over two by fours – an uncommon type of construction.

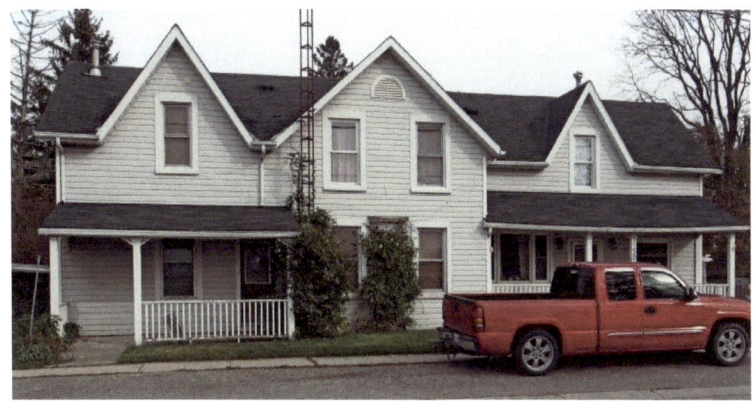

1150 Highway 54 – 1840 – This board and batten house was originally the Logan Hotel and was conveniently situated directly across from the original port of the Grand River Navigation Company. Crews from the river vessels and workers of the lumbering industries often stayed at this hotel.

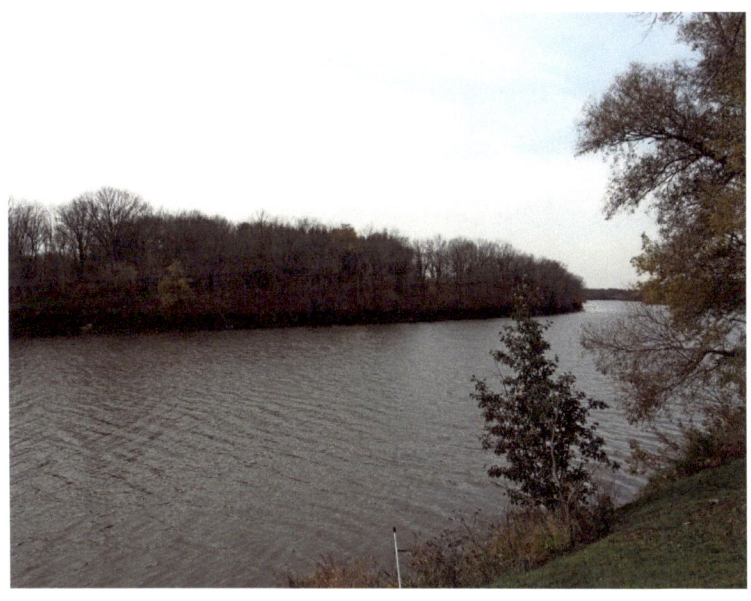

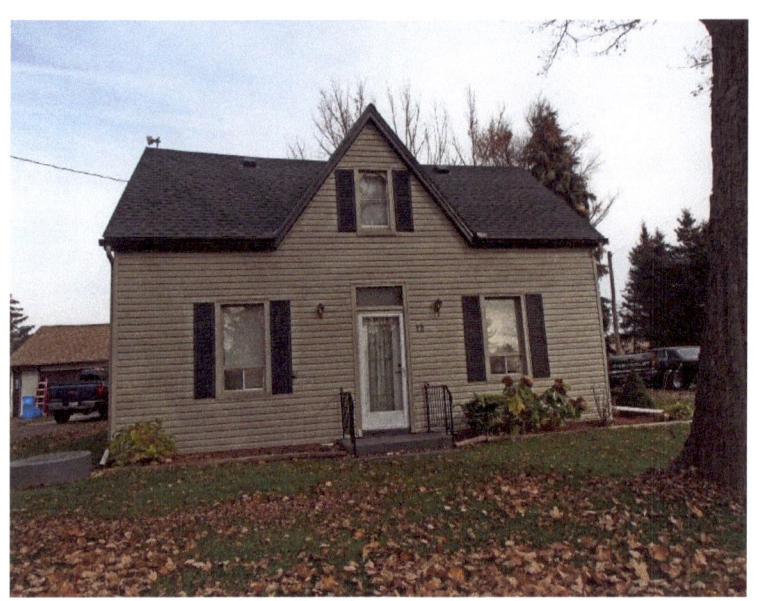

12 Middlepoint Road

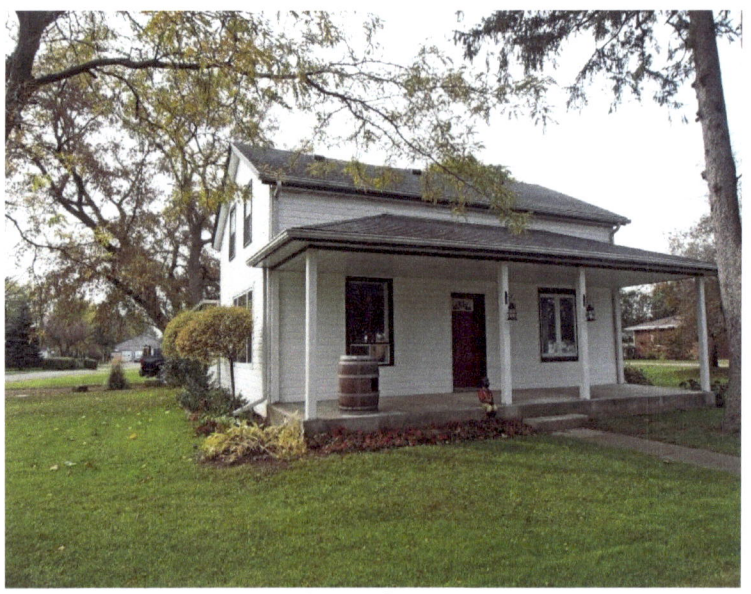

Hager Street

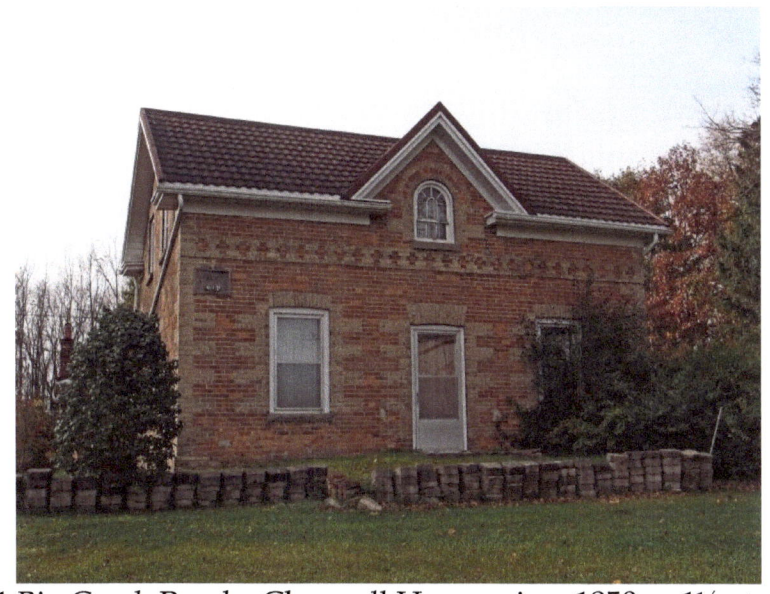

301 Big Creek Road – Cherwell House, circa 1850s – 1½-storey brick farmhouse – buff brick quoins on the corners, buff brick highlights around windows and door and a frieze at the top of the first storey elevation.

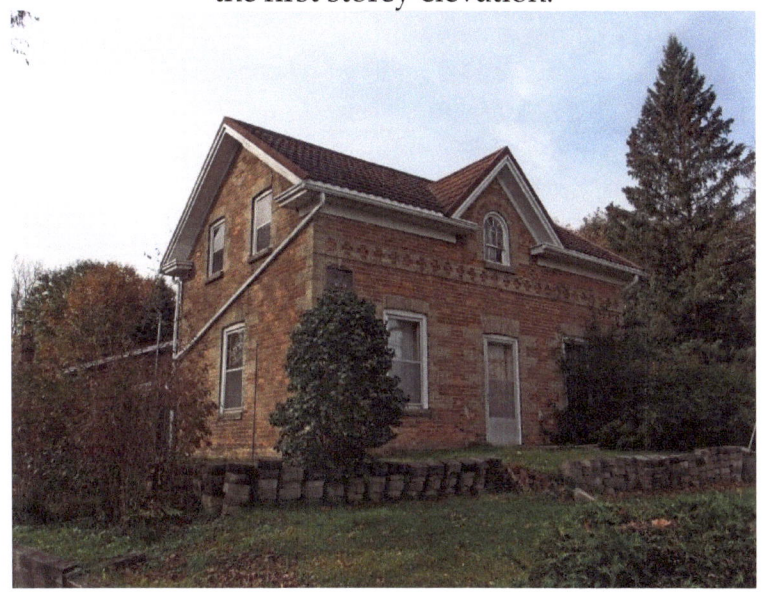

## Architectural Terms

| | |
|---|---|
| **Battlement:** A design for a parapet that has alternating solid parts and openings, originally used for defense, but later used as a decorative motif.<br>Example: 688 Mount Pleasant Road, Page 15 | 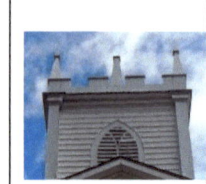 |
| **Bay Window:** A window that projects out from a wall, in a semicircular, rectangular, or polygonal design. Used frequently in Gothic and Victorian designs.<br>Example: 641 Mount Pleasant Road, Page 25 | 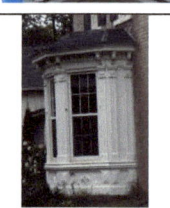 |
| **Belvedere**: (from the Italian "beautiful view") an architectural feature on a roof, in a garden or on a terrace that gives a beautiful view.<br>Example: 646 Mount Pleasant Road, Page 24 | 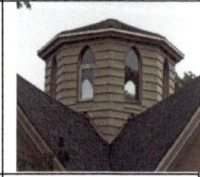 |
| **Brackets**: a decorative or weight-bearing structural element which forms a right angle with one side against a wall and the other under a projecting surface such as an eave or roof.<br>Example: 538 Mount Pleasant Road, Page 30 | 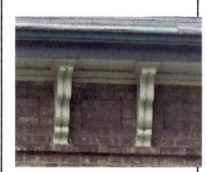 |
| **Buttress**: a masonry structure built against or projecting from a wall which serves to support or reinforce the wall. In Canadian architecture, they are sometimes used for decoration.<br>Example: 715 Mount Pleasant Road, Page 12 | 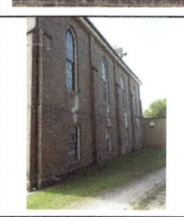 |
| **Capital:** The uppermost finish or decoration on a column. An Ionic column has a small base, a thin elegant shaft, and a capital composed of volutes which are carved whirls or twists that take the form of a scroll.<br>Example: 597 Mount Pleasant Road, Page 28 | 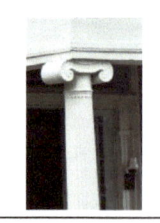 |

| | |
|---|---|
| **Cornice Return:** decorative element on the end of a gable.<br>Example: 660 Mount Pleasant Road, Page 22 | 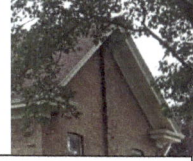 |
| **Dentil Moulding**: an even series of rectangles used as ornamental decoration in cornices.<br>Example: 669 Mount Pleasant Road, Page 20 | 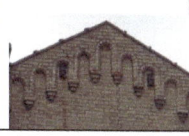 |
| **Dichromatic brickwork**: the use of two colours of brick, tile or slate to decorate a façade.<br>Example: 301 Big Creek Road, Page 64 | 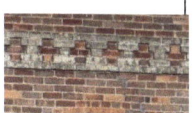 |
| **Dormer**: (French for "sleep") a gable end window that pierces through the plane of a sloping roof surface to create usable space in the top floor or attic of a building by adding headroom.<br>Example: 677 Mount Pleasant Road, Page 18 | 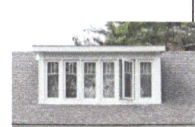 |
| **Entrance:** The entrance encompasses the doorway and the inner vestibule or, in residential architecture, the covered porch.<br>Example: 597 Mount Pleasant Road, Page 28 | 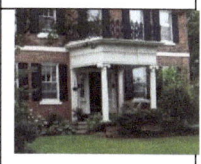 |
| **Gable**: the triangular portion of a wall between the edges of a sloping roof.<br><br>Example: 291 Baptist Church Road, Page 54 | 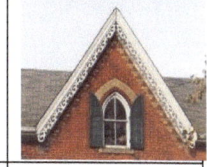 |
| **Gambrel Roof**: a symmetrical two-sided roof with two slopes on each side; the upper slope is positioned at a shallow angle, while the lower slope is steep. It is similar to a mansard roof, but a gambrel has vertical gable ends instead of being hipped at the four corners of the building.<br>Example: 670 Mount Pleasant Road, Page 19 | 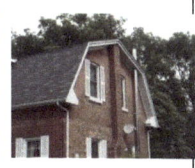 |

| | |
|---|---|
| **Hipped Roof**: a roof where all sides slope downwards to the walls with no gables. Example: Mount Pleasant Road, Page 14 | |
| **Iron Cresting**: A decorative ornament along the top of a roof. Iron cresting was popular in the Baroque era and also in Italianate, Victorian, Second Empire and Queen Anne styles of architecture. Example: 597 Mount Pleasant Road, Page 28 | |
| **Lancet Window**: a tall, narrow window with a pointed arch at its top. Example: 715 Mount Pleasant Road, Page 12 | |
| **Palladian Window**: a large window that is divided into three sections with the centre section larger than the two side sections and usually arched. Example: 421 Salt Springs Church Road, Page 47 | |
| **Pediment**: a triangular section above the door or portico, usually supported by columns. The inside of the triangle is called the tympanum. Example: 849 Mount Pleasant Road, Page 8 | |
| **Quoin**: masonry blocks at the corner of a wall, often a decorative feature, usually larger or of a different colour than the rest of the wall. Example: 518 Baptist Church Road, Page 51 | |

| | |
|---|---|
| **Sidelight**: a vertical window that flanks a door, and is often used to emphasize the importance of a primary entrance.<br>Example: 722 Mount Pleasant Road, Page 13 | 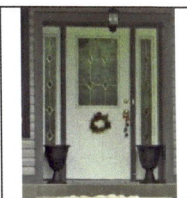 |
| **Tower:** A circular, square, or octagonal vertical structure higher than the surrounding structure that is usually part of an existing building and is created either for extra defense or for a specific purpose such as a clock or a bell tower.<br>Example: 1159 Highway 54, Page 61 | 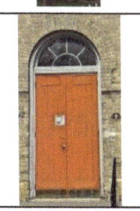 |
| **Transom Window:** the light above the doorway, also called a fanlight.<br><br>Example: 42 Brantford Street, Page 45 | |
| **Verge board and Finial**: also called bargeboards – hang from the projecting end of a roof and are often elaborately carved and ornamented. **Finial:** ornament added to the top of a gable, pinnacle, canopy or spire – a Gothic element.<br>Example: 641 Mount Pleasant Road, Page 25 | 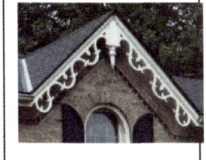 |
| **Window Hood:** A **hood** is the piece found above window openings, usually of an ornate design, and covers the top third of the opening. Hoods are commonly placed above arched or curved openings on both windows and doors.<br>Example: 538 Mount Pleasant Road, Page 30 | 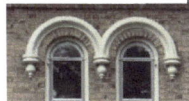 |

Building Styles

| | |
|---|---|
| **Edwardian**, 1900-1930 – This style bridges the ornate and elaborate styles of the Victorian era and the simplified styles of the 20th century. Edwardian Classicism provided simple, balanced facades, simple rooflines, dormer windows, large front porches, and smooth brick surfaces. Voussoirs and keystones are used sparingly and are understated. Finials and cresting are absent. Cornice brackets and braces are block-like and openings have flat arches or plain stone lintels.<br>Example: Centre Street, Onondaga, Page 46 | 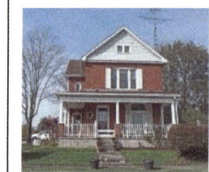 |
| **Georgian**, before 1860 – This style began with the British King Georges in the 18th century. These buildings have balanced facades around a central door, medium-pitched gable roofs, and small paned windows.<br>Example: 597 Mount Pleasant Road, Page 28 | 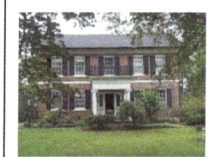 |
| **Gothic Revival**, 1830-1890 – These decorative buildings have sharply-pitched gables with highly detailed verge boards, pointed-arch window openings, and dichromatic brickwork. It is a common style in Ontario.<br>Example: 291 Baptist Church Road, Page 54 | 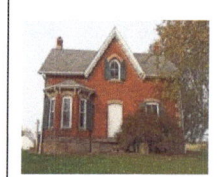 |
| **Italianate**, 1850-1900 – A two story rectangular building with a mild hip roof, a projecting frontispiece, and generous eaves with ornate cornice brackets was the basis of the style; often there are large sash windows, quoins, ornate detailing on the windows, and wraparound verandahs. Example: 1037 Highway 54, Onondaga, Page 42 | 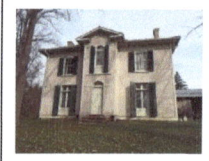 |

| | |
|---|---|
| **Neo-colonial** (also Colonial Revival, Georgian Revival or Neo-Georgian) architecture seeks to revive elements of architectural style of American colonial architecture of the period around the Revolutionary War which drew strongly from Georgian architecture of Great Britain. Architecture from the 18th and early 19th centuries in Ontario includes a wide assortment of detailing and ornament applied to a design centered around the fireplace and the source of water. Structures are typically two stories, have a symmetrical front facade with elaborate front doorways, often with decorative crown pediments, fanlights, and sidelights, symmetrical windows flanking the front entrance, often in pairs or threes, and columned porches.<br>Example: 670 Mount Pleasant Road, Page 19 | 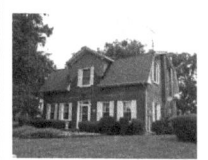 |
| **Neo-Gothic**: is monochromatic and on a much grander scale than Gothic. Early neo-Gothic churches were often plastered or painted, later neo-Gothic churches were not. An important moment in the development of neo-Gothic is the year 1853, when the hierarchy of the Roman Catholic church was fully restored in the Netherlands. Materials used were natural stone combined with brick. Around the year 1850 neo-Gothicism was maturing and increasingly became a Roman Catholic style almost exclusively. Wall buttresses and finials are added, but they are generally far too small to be of any structural benefit.<br>Example: 646 Mount Pleasant Road, Page 24 | 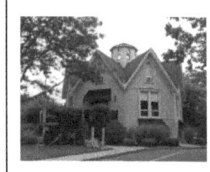 |

| | |
|---|---|
| **Regency Cottage**, 1830-1860 – This style originated in England in 1815 and spread to Ontario later in the 19th century as British officers retired to Canada. It is a modest one-storey house with a low-pitched hip roof and has a symmetrical front façade.<br>Example: 676 Mount Pleasant Road, Page 18 | |
| **Regency Style**, 1811-1820: Windows are tall and thin, with very small glazing bars separating the panes of glass. Balconies are of extremely fine ironwork, made of such delicate curves as to seem almost too frail to support the structure. Proportions are kept simple, with clean, classical lines. Windows and doors, particularly those on the ground floors, are often round-headed. Curved bow windows are popular, and often garden windows extended right down to the ground.<br>Example: 641 Mount Pleasant Road, Page 25 | |
| **Saltbox**: A saltbox is a building with a long, pitched roof that slopes down to the back, generally a wooden frame house. A saltbox has just one storey in the back and two stories in the front. The asymmetry of the unequal sides and the long, low rear roof line are the most distinctive features of a saltbox, which takes its name from its resemblance to a wooden lidded box in which salt was once kept. The earliest saltbox houses were created when a lean-to addition was added onto the rear of the original house extending the roof line sometimes to less than six feet from ground level.<br>Example: 664 Mount Pleasant Road, Page 21 | |

www.ingramcontent.com/pod-product-compliance
Lightning Source LLC
Chambersburg PA
CBHW040230220526
45473CB00001B/190